Congressional
Research Service

Informing the legislative debate since 1914

Federal Research and Development (R&D) Funding: FY2020

Updated March 18, 2020

Congressional Research Service

https://crsreports.congress.gov

R45715

Congressional Research Service

Informing the legislative debate since 1914

Federal Research and Development (R&D) Funding: FY2020

R45715

March 18, 2020

John F. Sargent Jr.,
Coordinator
Specialist in Science and
Technology Policy

President Trump's budget request for FY2020 included approximately $134.1 billion for research and development (R&D). Several FY2019 appropriations bills had not been enacted at the time the President's FY2020 budget was prepared; therefore, the President's budget included the FY2018 actual funding levels, 2019 annualized continuing resolution (CR) levels, and the FY2020 request levels. On February 15, 2019, Congress enacted the Consolidated Appropriations Act, 2019 (P.L. 116-6). This act included each of the remaining appropriations acts, completing the FY2019 appropriations process. The act also rendered the CR levels identified in the budget no longer relevant, though for some agencies the exact amount of R&D funding in the act remained uncertain. The analysis of government-wide R&D funding in this report compares the President's request for FY2020 to the FY2018 level.

In FY2018, OMB adopted a change to the definition of development, applying a more narrow treatment it describes as "experimental development." This change was intended to harmonize the reporting of U.S. R&D funding data with the approach used by other nations. The new definition is used in this report. Under the new definition of R&D (applied to both FY2018 and FY2020 figures), President Trump requested approximately $134.1 billion for R&D for FY2020, a decrease of $1.7 billion (1.2%) from the FY2018 level. Adjusted for inflation, the President's FY2020 R&D request represented a decrease of 5.1% below the FY2018 level.

Funding for R&D is concentrated in a few departments and agencies. In FY2018, eight federal agencies received 96.3% of total federal R&D funding, with the Department of Defense (DOD, 38.6%) and the Department of Health and Human Services (HHS, 27.2%) combined accounting for nearly two-thirds of all federal R&D funding. The same eight agencies accounted for 97.2% of the FY2020 request, with DOD accounting for 44.3% and HHS for 25.1%.

Under the President's FY2020 budget request, most federal agencies would have seen their R&D funding decline. The primary exception was the Department of Defense. DOD's requested R&D funding for FY2020 was $7.1 billion (13.5%) above the FY2018 level. The Departments of Transportation and Veterans Affairs would have seen small increases in R&D funding. Among the agencies with the largest proposed reductions in R&D funding in the FY2020 budget compared to the FY2018 actual levels were the Department of Energy ($2.8 billion, 15.8%), the National Science Foundation ($567 million, 9.0%), and National Aeronautics and Space Administration ($475 million, 4.0%).

The President's FY2020 budget request would have reduced funding for basic research by $1.5 billion (4.0%), applied research by $4.3 billion (10.5%), and facilities and equipment by $0.5 billion (12.8%), while increasing funding for development by $4.5 billion (8.3%). Budget supplements published after the President's FY2020 budget was released provide additional details for certain multiagency R&D initiatives. The President requested $5.506 billion for the Networking and Information Technology Research and Development (NITRD) program for FY2020, a decrease of $195 million (3.4%) over the estimated FY2019 level. The President requessted $1.469 billion for the National Nanotechnology Initiative for FY2020, a decrease of $103 million (6.6%) over the estimated FY2019 level. The FY2020 budget supplement for the U.S. Global Change Research Program has not yet been published. Some activities supporting these initiatives were discussed in agency budget justifications and are reported in the agency analyses in this report.

The request represents the President's R&D priorities. Congress may opt to agree with none, part, or all of the request, and it may express different priorities through the appropriations process. In recent years, Congress has completed the annual appropriations process after the start of the fiscal year. Completing the process after the start of the fiscal year and the accompanying use of continuing resolutions can affect agencies' execution of their R&D budgets, including the delay or cancellation of planned R&D activities and the acquisition of R&D-related equipment. As of the date of this report, Congress has enacted all 12 regular appropriations bills for FY2020. These bills were incorporated in two acts: the Consolidated Appropriations Act, 2020 (P.L. 116-93) and the Further Consolidated Appropriations Act, 2020 (P.L. 116-94). Both of these acts were signed into law on December 20,2019.

Contents

Figures

Tables

Appendixes

Contacts

Introduction

The 116th Congress continues its interest in U.S. research and development (R&D) and in evaluating support for federal R&D activities. The federal government has played an important role in supporting R&D efforts that have led to scientific breakthroughs and new technologies, from jet aircraft and the internet to communications satellites, shale gas extraction, and defenses against disease. In recent years, widespread concerns about the federal debt, recent and projected federal budget deficits, and federal budget caps have driven difficult decisions about the prioritization of R&D, both in the context of the entire federal budget and among competing needs within the federal R&D portfolio. Increases in the budget caps for FY2018 and FY2019 reduced some of the pressure affecting these decisions, but the concerns remain and the caps for FY2020 have not been increased.

The U.S. government supports a broad range of scientific and engineering R&D. Its purposes include specific concerns such as addressing national defense, health, safety, the environment, and energy security; advancing knowledge generally; developing the scientific and engineering workforce; and strengthening U.S. innovation and competitiveness in the global economy. Most of the R&D funded by the federal government is performed in support of the unique missions of individual funding agencies.

The federal R&D budget is an aggregation of the R&D activities of these agencies. There is no single, centralized source of R&D funds. Agency R&D budgets are developed internally as part of each agency's overall budget development process. R&D funding may be included either in accounts that are entirely devoted to R&D or in accounts that include funding for non-R&D activities. Agency budgets are subjected to review, revision, and approval by the Office of Management and Budget (OMB) and become part of the President's annual budget submission to Congress. The federal R&D budget is then calculated by aggregating the R&D activities of each federal agency.

Congress plays a central role in defining the nation's R&D priorities as it makes decisions about the level and allocation of R&D funding—overall, within agencies, and for specific programs. In recent years, some Members of Congress have expressed concerns about the level of federal spending (for R&D and for other purposes) in light of the federal deficit and debt. Other Members of Congress have expressed support for increased federal spending for R&D as an investment in the nation's future competitiveness. As Congress acted to complete the FY2020 appropriations process, it faced two overarching issues: the amount of the federal budget to be spent on federal R&D and the prioritization and allocation of the available funding.

This report begins with a discussion of the overall level of R&D in President Trump's FY2020 budget request, followed by analyses of R&D funding in the request from a variety of perspectives and for selected multiagency R&D initiatives. The remainder of the report discusses and analyzes the R&D budget requests of selected federal departments and agencies that, collectively, account for approximately 99% of total federal R&D funding.

Selected terms associated with federal R&D funding are defined in the text box on the next page. **Appendix A** provides a list of acronyms and abbreviations.

Definitions Associated with Federal Research and Development Funding

Two key sources of definitions associated with federal research and development funding are the White House Office of Management and Budget and the National Science Foundation.

Office of Management and Budget. The Office of Management and Budget provides the following definitions of R&D-related terms in OMB Circular No. A-11, "Preparation, Submission, and Execution of the Budget."[1] This document provides guidance to agencies in the preparation of the President's annual budget and instructions on budget execution. In 2017, OMB adopted a refinement to the categories of R&D, replacing "development" with "experimental development," which more narrowly defines the set of activities to be included. The new definition has resulted in lower reported R&D by some agencies, including the Department of Defense and the National Aeronautics and Space Administration. This definition is used in the President's FY2020 budget.

Conduct of R&D. Research and experimental development (R&D) activities are defined as creative and systematic work undertaken in order to increase the stock of knowledge—including knowledge of people, culture, and society—and to devise new applications using available knowledge.

Basic Research. Basic research is defined as experimental or theoretical work undertaken primarily to acquire new knowledge of the underlying foundations of phenomena and observable facts. Basic research may include activities with broad or general applications in mind, such as the study of how plant genomes change, but should exclude research directed towards a specific application or requirement, such as the optimization of the genome of a specific crop species.

Applied Research. Applied research is defined as original investigation undertaken in order to acquire new knowledge. Applied research is, however, directed primarily towards a specific practical aim or objective.

Experimental Development. Experimental development is defined as creative and systematic work, drawing on knowledge gained from research and practical experience, which is directed at producing new products or processes or improving existing products or processes. Like research, experimental development will result in gaining additional knowledge.

R&D Equipment. R&D equipment includes amounts for major equipment for research and development. It includes acquisition, design, or production of major movable equipment, such as mass spectrometers, research vessels, DNA sequencers, and other major movable instruments for use in R&D activities. It includes programs of $1 million or more that are devoted to the purchase or construction of major R&D equipment

R&D Facilities. R&D facilities includes amounts for the construction of facilities that are necessary for the execution of an R&D program. This may include land, major fixed equipment, and supporting infrastructure such as a sewer line or housing at a remote location.

National Science Board/National Science Foundation. The National Science Board/National Science Foundation provides the following definitions of R&D-related terms in its *Science and Engineering Indicators: 2018* report.[2]

Research and Development (R&D): Research and experimental development comprise creative and systematic work undertaken to increase the stock of knowledge—including knowledge of humankind, culture, and society—and its use to devise new applications of available knowledge.

Basic Research: Experimental or theoretical work undertaken primarily to acquire new knowledge of the underlying foundations of phenomena and observable facts, without any particular application or use in view.

Applied Research: Original investigation undertaken to acquire new knowledge; directed primarily, however, toward a specific, practical aim or objective.

Experimental Development: Systematic work, drawing on knowledge gained from research and practical experience and producing additional knowledge, which is directed to producing new products or processes or to improving existing products or processes.

---

[1] The White House, Office of Management and Budget, Circular No. A-11, "Preparation, Submission, and Execution of the Budget," June 2018, https://www.whitehouse.gov/wp-content/uploads/2018/06/a11.pdf.

[2] National Science Board/National Science Foundation, *Science and Engineering Indicators 2018*, January 2018, https://www.nsf.gov/statistics/2018/nsb20181/.

The President's FY2020 Budget Request

On March 11, 2019, President Trump released his proposed FY2020 budget. He provided additional details the following week.

Completion of the FY2019 budget process on February 15, 2019, more than four months after the start of FY2019, as well as a government shutdown, led to both a delay in the scheduled release of the President's FY2020 budget request, and the use by the Office of Management and Budget of a mix of estimated continuing appropriations act FY2019 funding levels (generally, for agencies whose FY2019 appropriations were enacted after the start of FY2019)[3] and enacted FY2019 funding levels (generally, for agencies whose appropriations were enacted prior to the start of FY2019).[4] As a result, the aggregate (total) FY2019 R&D funding levels for all agencies in the *Analytical Perspectives* addendum to the President's FY2020 budget were estimated "using FY 2019 enacted appropriations where available and annualized Continuing Resolution [levels] for agencies without enacted appropriations prior to Feb. 15, 2019."[5] With enactment of the remaining FY2019 appropriations acts in the Consolidated Appropriations Act, 2019 (P.L. 116-6), the Administration's estimated aggregate R&D funding level no longer accurately reflected total enacted FY2019 R&D funding. OMB did not issue a document with comprehensive R&D figures for each agency or in aggregate until the February 2020 release of the President's FY2021 budget.

Therefore, the analysis of government-wide R&D funding in this report compares the President's request for FY2020 to the FY2018 actual level. As information about the agencies' FY2019 R&D levels became available, the agency sections of this report were updated to reflect that information and to make comparisons to the President's FY2020 request.

President Trump proposed approximately $134.1 billion for R&D for FY2020, $1.7 billion (1.2%) below the FY2018 level of $135.8 billion. Adjusted for inflation, the President's FY2020 R&D request represented a constant-dollar decrease of 5.2% from the FY2018 actual level.[6]

The President's request included continued R&D funding for existing single-agency and multiagency programs and activities, as well as new initiatives. This report provides government-wide, multiagency, and individual agency analyses of the President's FY2020 request as it relates to R&D and related activities, as well as Congressional actions on FY2020 appropriations.

---

[3] Agencies that received their FY2019 appropriations in the Consolidated Appropriations Act, 2019 (P.L. 116-6).

[4] Agencies that received their FY2019 appropriations in the Energy and Water, Legislative Branch, and Military Construction and Veterans Affairs Appropriations Act, 2019 (P.L. 115-244), and the Department of Defense and Labor, Health and Human Services, and Education Appropriations Act, 2019 and Continuing Appropriations Act, 2019 (P.L. 115-245).

[5] Executive Office of the President (EOP), OMB, *Analytical Perspectives, Budget of the United States Government, Fiscal Year 2020, Research and Development,* March 18, 2019, p. 269, https://www.whitehouse.gov/wp-content/uploads/2019/03/ap_21_research-fy2020.pdf.

[6] As calculated by CRS using the Gross Domestic Product (GDP) (chained) price index for FY2018 and FY2020 in Table 10.1, "Gross Domestic Product and Deflators Used in the Historical Tables: 1940–2022," *Budget of the United States Government, Fiscal Year 2019*, https://www.whitehouse.gov/wp-content/uploads/2018/02/hist10z1-fy2019.xlsx.

Other Factors Affecting Analysis of the FY2019 Budget Request

Other factors complicate the analysis of changes in R&D funding for FY2019, both in aggregate and for selected agencies. For example:

- Beginning in FY2018, OMB replaced the R&D category "development" with a subset referred to as "experimental development" in an effort that OMB asserts better aligns its data with the survey data collected by the National Science Foundation, and for greater consistency with international standards. The new definition excludes some development activities, primarily at the Department of Defense (DOD) and the National Aeronautics and Space Administration (NASA) that had been characterized as development in previous budgets. The new definition (experimental development) is used throughout this report for FY2017 and later years, except in the section "Department of Defense," which treats non-experimental development funding as part of its total research, development, testing, and evaluation budget in line with DOD practice.

- Inconsistency among agencies in the reporting of R&D and the inclusion of R&D activities in accounts with non-R&D activities may result in different figures being reported by OMB and the White House Office of Science and Technology Policy (OSTP), including those shown in Table 1, and those in agency budget analyses that appear later in this report.

Federal R&D Funding Perspectives

Federal R&D funding can be analyzed from a variety of perspectives that provide different insights. The following sections examine the data by agency, by the character of the work supported, and by a combination of these two perspectives.

Federal R&D by Agency

Congress makes decisions about R&D funding through the authorization and appropriations processes primarily from the perspective of individual agencies and programs. **Table 1** provides data on R&D funding by agency for FY2018 (actual), FY2019 (enacted, for selected agencies), and FY2020 (request).[7] Enacted data for FY2019 is provided only for agencies whose FY2019 appropriations process was completed before the FY2020 budget request was finalized.

Congress completed action on FY2020 appropriations with passage of two consolidated appropriations acts on December 22, 2019: the Consolidated Appropriations Act, 2020 (P.L. 116-93) and the Further Consolidated Appropriations Act, 2020 (P.L. 116-94). These two acts together incorporated the 12 regular appropriations acts. The following section presents the President's FY2020 request. Enacted appropriations are presented in the agency sections that follow.

Under the request, eight federal agencies would have received more than 97% of total federal R&D funding in FY2020: the Department of Defense, 44.3%; Department of Health and Human Services (HHS), primarily the National Institutes of Health (NIH), 25.1%; Department of Energy (DOE), 11.0%; National Aeronautics and Space Administration, 8.4%; National Science Foundation (NSF), 4.3%; Department of Agriculture (USDA), 1.8%; Department of Commerce (DOC), 1.3%; and Department of Veterans Affairs (VA), 1.0%. This report provides an analysis of the R&D budget requests for these agencies, as well as for the Department of Homeland Security (DHS), Department of the Interior (DOI), Department of Transportation (DOT), and Environmental Protection Agency (EPA).

---

[7] EOP, OMB, *Analytical Perspectives, Budget of the United States Government, Fiscal Year 2020, Research and Development,* March 18, 2019, p. 269, https://www.whitehouse.gov/wp-content/uploads/2019/03/ap_21_research-fy2020.pdf.

All but three federal agencies would have seen their R&D funding decrease under the President's FY2020 request compared to FY2018. The only agencies that would have seen increased R&D funding in FY2020 relative to the FY2018 level were DOD (up $7.077 billion, 13.5%), VA (up $39 million, 3.0%), and DOT (up $33 million, 3.2%). The agencies with largest R&D funding declines in the FY2020 request compared to FY2018 (as measured in dollars) were in the budgets of HHS (down $3.249 billion, 8.8%), DOE (down $2.764 billion, 15.8%), NSF (down $567 million, 29.7%), and NASA (down $475 million, 4.0%).

Among agencies for which FY2019 enacted funding is shown in the President's budget, FY2020 R&D funding would have increased only for DOD (up $3.631 billion, 6.5%). HHS R&D funding would have declined by $4.954 billion (12.8%). DOE R&D funding would have declined by $3.075 billion (17.3%). VA R&D funding would have declined by $17 million (1.3%). Department of Education R&D funding would have declined by $34 million (13.2%). See **Table 1**.

Table 1. Federal Research and Development Funding by Agency, FY2018-FY2020

(budget authority, dollar amounts in millions)

Department/Agency	FY2018 Actual	FY2019 Enacted	FY2020 Request	Change, FY2018-FY2020		Change, FY2019-FY2020	
				Dollar	Percent, Total	Dollar	Percent, Total
Department of Defense	$52,386	$55,832	$59,463	$7,077	13.5%	$3,631	6.5%
Dept. of Health and Human Services	36,942	38,647	33,693	-3,249	-8.8%	-4,954	-12.8%
Department of Energy	17,482	17,793	14,718	-2,764	-15.8%	-3,075	-17.3%
NASA	11,755	n/a	11,280	-475	-4.0%	n/a	n/a
National Science Foundation	6,327	n/a	5,760	-567	-9.0%	n/a	n/a
Department of Agriculture	2,618	n/a	2,464	-154	-5.9%	n/a	n/a
Department of Commerce	2,029	n/a	1,694	-335	-16.5%	n/a	n/a
Department of Veterans Affairs	1,286	1,342	1,325	39	3.0%	17	-1.3%
Department of Transportation	1,043	n/a	1,076	33	3.2%	n/a	n/a
Department of the Interior	885	n/a	753	-132	-14.9%	n/a	n/a
Department of Homeland Security	725	n/a	507	-218	-30.1%	n/a	n/a
Environmental Protection Agency	492	n/a	285	-207	-42.1%	n/a	n/a
Smithsonian Institution	357	n/a	315	-42	-11.8%	n/a	n/a
Department of Education	257	258	224	-33	-12.8%	34	-13.2%
Other	1,181	n/a	540	-641	-54.3%	n/a	n/a
Total	**135,765**	**n/a**	**134,097**	**-1,668**	**-1.2%**	**n/a**	**n/a**

Source: CRS analysis of data from EOP, OMB, *Analytical Perspectives, Budget of the United States Government, Fiscal Year 2020, Research and Development,* March 18, 2019, p. 269, https://www.whitehouse.gov/wp-content/uploads/2019/03/ap_21_research-fy2020.pdf. The "FY2019" column includes enacted funding levels for only those agencies that received appropriations prior to February 15, 2019, for which OMB provided estimated levels of R&D based on the enacted legislation.

Notes: Components may not sum to totals due to rounding. n/a = not available.

Federal R&D by Character of Work, Facilities, and Equipment

Federal R&D funding can also be examined by the character of work it supports—basic research, applied research, or development—and by funding provided for construction of R&D facilities and acquisition of major R&D equipment. (See **Table 2.**) President Trump's FY2020 request included $35.164 billion for basic research, down $1.452 billion (4.0%) from FY2018; $40.707 billion for applied research, down $4.264 billion (10.5%); $59.108 billion for development, up $4.543 billion (8.3%); and $3.382 billion for facilities and equipment, down $495 million (12.8%).

Table 2. Federal R&D Funding by Character of Work and Facilities and Equipment, FY2018 and FY2020

(budget authority, dollar amounts in millions)

Character of Work, Facilities, and Equipment	FY2018 Actual	FY2020 Request	Change, FY2018-FY2020	
			Dollars	**Percent**
Basic research	36,616	35,164	-1,452	-4.0%
Applied research	40,707	36,443	-4,264	-10.5%
Development	54,565	59,108	4,543	8.3%
Facilities and Equipment	3,877	3,382	-495	-12.8%
Total	**135,765**	**134,097**	**-1,668**	**-1.2%**

Source: CRS analysis of data from EOP, OMB, *Analytical Perspectives, Budget of the United States Government, Fiscal Year 2020, Research and Development,* March 18, 2019, pp. 271-272, https://www.whitehouse.gov/wp-content/uploads/2019/03/ap_21_research-fy2020.pdf.

Note: Components may not sum to totals due to rounding.

Federal Role in U.S. R&D by Character of Work

A primary policy justification for public investments in basic research and for incentives (e.g., tax credits) for the private sector to conduct research is the view, widely held by economists, that the private sector will, left on its own, underinvest in basic research from a societal perspective. The usual argument for this view is that the social returns (i.e., the benefits to society at large) exceed the private returns (i.e., the benefits accruing to the private investor, such as increased revenues or higher stock value). Other factors that may inhibit corporate investment in basic research include long time horizons for achieving commercial applications (diminishing the potential returns due to the time value of money), high levels of technical risk/uncertainty, shareholder demands for shorter-term returns, and asymmetric and imperfect information.

The federal government is the nation's largest supporter of basic research, funding 42% of U.S. basic research in 2017. Business funded 30% of U.S. basic research in 2017, with state governments, universities, and other nonprofit organizations funding the remaining 29%. For U.S. applied research, business is the primary funder, accounting for an estimated 55% in 2017, while the federal government accounted for an estimated 33%. State governments, universities, and other nonprofit organizations funded the remaining 12%. Business also provides the vast majority of U.S. funding for development. Business accounted for 85% of development funding in 2017, while the federal government provided 13%. State governments, universities, and other nonprofit organizations funded the remaining 2% (see **Figure 1**).[8]

Figure 1. Composition of U.S. Basic Research, Applied Research, and Development by Funding Sector, 2017

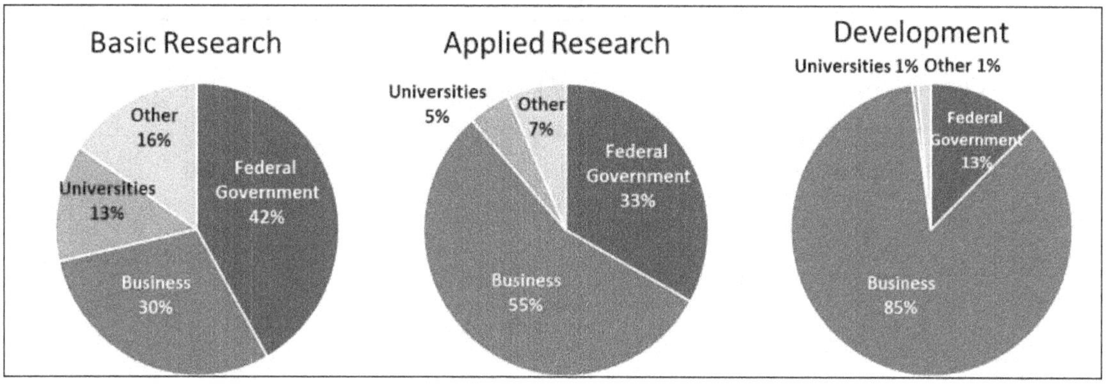

Source: CRS analysis of National Science Foundation, *National Patterns of R&D Resources: 2016–17 Data Update,* NSF 19-309, February 27, 2019, https://ncses.nsf.gov/pubs/nsf19309/.

Notes: Components may not add to total due to rounding. Data for 2017 are estimated and subject to revision.

Federal R&D by Agency and Character of Work Combined

Federal R&D funding can also be viewed from the combined perspective of each agency's contribution to basic research, applied research, development, and facilities and equipment. **Table 3** lists the three agencies with the most funding in each of these categories as proposed in the President's FY2020 budget. The overall federal R&D budget reflects a wide range of national priorities, including supporting advances in spaceflight, developing new and affordable sources of energy, and understanding and deterring terrorist groups. These priorities and the mission of each individual agency contribute to the composition of that agency's R&D spending (i.e., the allocation among basic research, applied research, development, and facilities and equipment). In the President's FY2020 budget request, the Department of Health and Human Services, primarily NIH, would have accounted for nearly half (47.7%) of all federal funding for basic research. HHS would have also been the largest federal funder of applied research, accounting for about 45.6% of all federally funded applied research in the President's FY2020 budget request. DOD would have been the primary federal funder of development, accounting for 87.4% of total federal development funding in the President's FY2020 budget request. DOE would have been the primary federal funder of facilities and equipment, accounting for 50.5% of total federal facilities and equipment funding in the President's FY2020 budget request.[9]

---

[8] CRS analysis of National Science Foundation, *National Patterns of R&D Resources: 2016–17 Data Update*, NSF 19-309, February 27, 2019, https://ncses.nsf.gov/pubs/nsf19309/. Components may not add to total due to rounding.

[9] EOP, OMB, *Analytical Perspectives, Budget of the United States Government, Fiscal Year 2019,* February 12, 2018, pp. 238-240, https://www.whitehouse.gov/omb/budget/Analytical_Perspectives.

Table 3. Selected R&D Funding Agencies by Character of Work, Facilities, and Equipment, FY2018 Actual and FY2020 Request

(budget authority, dollar amounts in millions)

Character of Work/Agency	FY2018 Actual	FY2020 Request	Change, FY2018-FY2020	
			Dollars	Percent
Basic Research				
Health and Human Services	18,278	16,785	-1,493	-8.2%
Energy	5,005	4,647	-358	-7.2%
National Science Foundation	5,066	4,568	-498	-9.8%
Applied Research				
Health and Human Services	18,414	16,624	-1,790	-9.7%
Energy	7,998	6,410	-1,588	-19.9%
Defense	5,690	5,440	-250	-4.4%
Experimental Development				
Defense	44,363	51,686	7,323	16.5%
NASA	5,872	3,791	-2,081	-35.4%
Energy	2,549	1,952	-597	-23.4%
Facilities and Equipment				
Energy	1,930	1,709	-221	-11.5%
Commerce	633	566	-67	-10.6%
National Science Foundation	503	505	2	0.4%

Source: CRS analysis of data from EOP, OMB, *Analytical Perspectives, Budget of the United States Government, Fiscal Year 2020, Research and Development,* March 18, 2019, pp. 271-272, https://www.whitehouse.gov/wp-content/uploads/2019/03/ap_21_research-fy2020.pdf.

Note: This table shows only the top three funding agencies in each category, based on the FY2020 request.

Multiagency R&D Initiatives

For many years, presidential budgets have reported on multiagency R&D initiatives. Often, they have also provided details of agency funding for these initiatives. Some of these efforts have a statutory basis—for example, the Networking and Information Technology Research and Development (NITRD) program, the National Nanotechnology Initiative (NNI), and the U.S. Global Change Research Program (USGCRP). These programs generally produce annual budget supplements identifying objectives, activities, funding levels, and other information, usually published shortly after the presidential budget release. Other multiagency R&D initiatives have operated at the discretion of the President without such a basis and may be eliminated at the discretion of the President. President Trump's FY2020 budget was largely silent on funding levels for these efforts and whether any or all of the nonstatutory initiatives will continue. Some activities related to these initiatives were discussed in agency budget justifications and may be addressed in the agency analyses later in this report. This section provides available multiagency information on these initiatives.

Networking and Information Technology Research and Development Program (NITRD)

Established by the High-Performance Computing Act of 1991 (P.L. 102-194), the Networking and Information Technology Research and Development program is the primary mechanism by which the federal government coordinates its unclassified networking and information technology R&D investments in areas such as supercomputing, high-speed networking, cybersecurity, software engineering, and information management. According to NITRD, it coordinates the information technology R&D activities of 24 federal agency members and more than 45 other participating agencies with program interests and activities in IT R&D. NITRD efforts are coordinated by the National Science and Technology Council (NSTC) Subcommittee on Networking and Information Technology Research and Development.[10]

P.L. 102-194, as reauthorized by the American Innovation and Competitiveness Act of 2017 (P.L. 114-329), requires the director of NITRD to prepare an annual report to be delivered to Congress along with the President's budget request. This annual report, often referred to as a budget supplement, is to include, among other things, detailed information on the program's budget for the current and previous fiscal years and the proposed budget for the next fiscal year. The latest annual report was published in September 2019 and related to the FY2020 budget request. President Trump requested $5.506 billion for NITRD research in FY2020, a decrease of $195 million (3.4%) from the estimated FY2019 level.[11]

For additional information on the NITRD program, see CRS Report RL33586, *The Federal Networking and Information Technology Research and Development Program: Background, Funding, and Activities*, by Patricia Moloney Figliola. Additional NITRD information also can be obtained at https://www.nitrd.gov.

Table 4. Networking and Information Technology Research and Development Program Funding, FY2018-FY2020

(budget authority, in millions of current dollars)

FY2018 Actual	FY2019 Estimate	FY2020 Request
$5,310.5	$5,700.5	$5,505.8

Source: EOP, National Science and Technology Council, *The Networking and Information Technology Research and Development Program: Supplement to the President's FY2020 Budget,* September 2019.

---

[10] The NSTC was established by Executive Order 12881 in 1993. According to the White House, "This Cabinet-level Council is the principal means within the Executive Branch to coordinate science and technology policy across the diverse entities that make up the Federal research and development enterprise. Chaired by the President, the membership of the NSTC is made up of the Vice President, Cabinet Secretaries and Agency Heads with significant science and technology responsibilities, and other White House officials. In practice, the Assistant to the President for Science and Technology Policy oversees the NSTC's ongoing activities." (Source: The White House, Office of Science and Technology Policy, "NSTC," https://www.whitehouse.gov/ostp/nstc/.) For more information on the NSTC, see CRS Report R43935, *Office of Science and Technology Policy (OSTP): History and Overview*, by John F. Sargent Jr. and Dana A. Shea; and https://www.whitehouse.gov/ostp/nstc/.

[11] EOP, National Science and Technology Council, *The Networking and Information Technology Research and Development Program: Supplement to the President's FY2020 Budget,* September 2019.

U.S. Global Change Research Program (USGCRP)

The U.S. Global Change Research Program coordinates and integrates federal research and applications to understand, assess, predict, and respond to human-induced and natural processes of global change. The program seeks to advance global climate change science and to "build a knowledge base that informs human responses to climate and global change through coordinated and integrated Federal programs of research, education, communication, and decision support."[12] In FY2018, 13 departments and agencies participated in the USGCRP. USGCRP efforts are coordinated by the NSTC Subcommittee on Global Change Research. Each agency develops and carries out its activities as its contribution to the USGCRP, and funds are appropriated to each agency for those activities; those activities may or may not be identified as associated with the USGCRP in the President's annual budget proposal or each agency's budget justification.

The Global Change Research Act of 1990 (GCRA) (P.L. 101-606) requires each federal agency or department involved in global change research to report annually to Congress on each element of its proposed global change research activities, as well as the portion of its budget request allocated to each element of the program.[13] The President is also required to identify those activities and the annual global change research budget in the President's annual budget request.

In addition, in almost each of the past 17 years, language in appropriations laws has required the President to submit a comprehensive report to the appropriations committees "describing in detail all Federal agency funding, domestic and international, for climate change programs, projects, and activities ... including an accounting of funding by agency...."[14] **Table 5** presents data from *Our Changing Planet: The U.S. Global Change Research Program for Fiscal Years 2018-2019*, the President's most recent report. This section will be updated when the USGCRP updates its budget information.

For additional information on the USGCRP, see CRS Report R43227, *Federal Climate Change Funding from FY2008 to FY2014*, by Jane A. Leggett, Richard K. Lattanzio, and Emily Bruner. Additional USGCRP information also can be obtained at http://www.globalchange.gov.

Table 5. U.S. Global Change Research Program Funding, FY2018-FY2020

(budget authority, in millions of current dollars)

	FY2018 Enacted	FY2019 Request	FY2020 Request
Total, USGCRP	**$2,546**	**$2,013**	**TBD**

Sources: U.S. Global Change Research Program, *Our Changing Planet: The U.S. Global Change Research Program for Fiscal Years 2018-2019*, 2019, p. 29. https://downloads.globalchange.gov/ocp/ocp2018/Our-Changing-Planet_FY-2018-2019.pdf.

Notes: TBD = to be determined. Funding for the USGCRP is appropriated to more than a dozen federal departments and agencies, and some spending of it is transferred or coordinated through interagency agreements. Almost all of the funding is spent directly by agencies on research and related activities; a small percentage is spent for interagency coordination and communications in the USGCRP program office.

---

[12] U.S. Global Change Research Program website, http://www.globalchange.gov/about/mission-vision-strategic-plan..

[13] Directives to report annually to Congress on budget requests and spending occur in several sections of P.L. 101-606, including Sections 105(b) and (c) on Budget Coordination, and Section 107, Annual Report.

[14] See, most recently, P.L. 115-31, Consolidated Appropriations Act, 2017, Section 416.

National Nanotechnology Initiative (NNI)

Launched in FY2001, the National Nanotechnology Initiative is a multiagency R&D initiative to advance understanding and control of matter at the nanoscale, where the physical, chemical, and biological properties of materials differ in fundamental and useful ways from the properties of individual atoms or bulk matter.[15] In 2003, Congress enacted the 21st Century Nanotechnology Research and Development Act (P.L. 108-153), providing a legislative foundation for some of the activities of the NNI. NNI efforts are coordinated by the NSTC Subcommittee on Nanoscale Science, Engineering, and Technology (NSET). For FY2020, the President's request included NNI funding for 15 federal departments and independent agencies and commissions with budgets dedicated to nanotechnology R&D. The NSET includes other federal departments and independent agencies and commissions with responsibilities for health, safety, and environmental regulation; trade; education; intellectual property; international relations; and other areas that might affect or be affected by nanotechnology.

P.L. 108-153 requires the NSTC to prepare an annual report to be delivered to Congress at the time the President's budget request is sent to Congress. This annual report, often referred to as a budget supplement, is to include detailed information on the program's budget for the current fiscal year and the program's proposed budget for the next fiscal year, as well as additional information and data related to the performance of the program. The latest annual report was published in August 2019 and related to the FY2020 budget request. President Trump requested $1,469 billion for NNI research in FY2020, a decrease of $103 million (6.6%) from the estimated FY2019 level.[16]

For additional information on the NNI, see CRS Report RL34401, *The National Nanotechnology Initiative: Overview, Reauthorization, and Appropriations Issues*, by John F. Sargent Jr. Additional NNI information also can be obtained at http://www.nano.gov.

Table 6. National Nanotechnology Initiative Funding, FY2018-FY2020

(budget authority, in millions of current dollars)

FY2018 Actual	FY2019 Estimated	FY2020 Request
$1.740.9	$1,572.1	$1,468.7

Source: EOP, National Science and Technology Council, *The National Nanotechnology Initiative: Supplement to the President's 2020 Budget*, August 2019.

American Artificial Intelligence Initiative

In February 2019, President Trump signed Executive Order 13859 establishing an American Artificial Intelligence Initiative to accelerate national leadership in artificial intelligence (AI).[17] Among other things, the EO directs the heads of implementing agencies that perform or fund

---

[15] In the context of the NNI and nanotechnology, the nanoscale refers to lengths of 1 to 100 nanometers. A nanometer is one-billionth of a meter, or about the width of 10 hydrogen atoms arranged side by side in a line.

[16] EOP, National Science and Technology Council, *The National Nanotechnology Initiative: Supplement to the President's 2020 Budget*, August 2019.

[17] Executive Order 13859, "Maintaining American Leadership in Artificial Intelligence," 84 *Federal Register* 3967-3972, February 11, 2019, https://www.federalregister.gov/documents/2019/02/14/2019-02544/maintaining-american-leadership-in-artificial-intelligence.

R&D to consider AI as an agency R&D priority, in accordance with their missions and consistent with applicable law. In particular, the EO directs the Secretaries of Defense, Commerce, Health and Human Services, and Energy, the Administrator of the National Aeronautics and Space Administration, and the Director of the National Science Foundation to prioritize the allocation of high-performance computing resources for AI-related applications through increased assignment of discretionary funding and any other appropriate mechanisms. According to *Analytical Perspectives,* the President's FY2020 budget would have provided approximately $850 million for this initiative to the Department of Energy, National Institutes of Health, National Institute of Standards and Technology, and National Science Foundation.[18]

National Quantum Initiative

In December 2018, President Trump signed the National Quantum Initiative Act (P.L. 115-368) establishing a National Quantum Initiative with the stated purpose of ensuring "the continued leadership of the United States in quantum information science [QIS] and its technology applications." The act requires the establishment of a 10-year plan to accelerate the development of QIS and technology applications. According to *Analytical Perspectives*, the President's FY2020 budget included approximately $430 million for this initiative at DOD, DOE, NIST, and NSF.[19]

Other Initiatives

A number of presidential initiatives without statutory foundations were in operation at the end of the Obama Administration, but have not been addressed explicitly in President Trump's FY2018, FY2019, or FY2020 budgets. Two of these are part of the Advanced Manufacturing Partnership (AMP): the National Robotics Initiative (NRI) and Manufacturing USA (formerly known as the National Network for Manufacturing Innovation or NNMI).[20]

According to *Analytical Perspectives*, the President's FY2020 budget

> prioritizes R&D aimed at advances in manufacturing and the integration of those advances into the domestic supply chain to reduce U.S. reliance on foreign sources of critical products. Budget priorities include intelligent manufacturing systems, materials and processing technologies, advances in semiconductor design and fabrication, and innovations in food and agricultural manufacturing.[21]

Other initiatives include the Cancer Moonshot, the Brain Research through Advancing Innovative Neurotechnologies (BRAIN) Initiative, the Precision Medicine Initiative (PMI), the Materials Genome Initiative (MGI), and an effort to double federal funding for clean energy R&D. Some of

---

[18] EOP, OMB, *Analytical Perspectives, Budget of the United States Government, Fiscal Year 2020, Research and Development,* March 18, 2019, pp. 269, https://www.whitehouse.gov/wp-content/uploads/2019/03/ap_21_research-fy2020.pdf

[19] Ibid., p. 270.

[20] Funding for Manufacturing USA is requested in the National Institute of Standards and Technology (NIST) and Department of Defense budget justifications. NIST's FY2020 budget justification requests $15.2 million to support the National Institute for Innovation in Manufacturing Biopharmaceuticals (NIIMBL, approximately $10 million), which was competed and selected by NIST, and for the Manufacturing USA network (approximately $5 million). In addition, the Department of Defense is requesting $66.2 million for FY2020 for the DOD-sponsored institutes that are part of the Manufacturing USA network as part of the request of the Office of the Secretary of Defense (see DOD program element 0603680D8Z).

[21] EOP, OMB, *Analytical Perspectives, Budget of the United States Government, Fiscal Year 2020, Research and Development,* March 18, 2019, p. 270.

---

the activities of these initiatives are discussed in agency budget justifications and the agency analyses later in this report.

FY2020 Appropriations Status

The remainder of this report provides a more in-depth analysis of R&D in 12 federal departments and agencies that, in aggregate, receive nearly 99% of total federal R&D funding. Agencies are presented in order of the size of their FY2020 R&D budget requests, with the largest presented first.

Annual appropriations for these agencies are provided through 9 of the 12 regular appropriations bills. For each agency covered in this report, **Table 7** shows the corresponding regular appropriations bill that provides primary funding for the agency, including its R&D activities.

Because of the way that agencies report budget data to Congress, it can be difficult to identify the portion that is R&D. Consequently, R&D data presented in the agency analyses in this report may differ from R&D data in the President's budget or otherwise provided by OMB.

Funding for R&D is often included in appropriations line items that also include non-R&D activities; therefore, in such cases, it may not be possible to identify precisely how much of the funding provided in appropriations laws is allocated to R&D specifically. In general, R&D funding levels are known only after departments and agencies allocate their appropriations to specific activities and report those figures.

Congress completed action on FY2020 appropriations with passage of two consolidated appropriations acts on December 19, 2019: the Consolidated Appropriations Act, 2020 (P.L. 116-93) and the Further Consolidated Appropriations Act, 2020 (P.L. 116-94). These two acts together incorporated the 12 regular appropriations acts. President Trump signed these bills into law on December 20, 2019.

In addition to this report, CRS produces individual reports on each of the appropriations bills and for a number of federal agencies. These reports can be accessed via the CRS website at http://www.crs.gov/iap/appropriations. Also, the status of each appropriations bill is available on the CRS web page, *Status Table of Appropriations*, available at http://www.crs.gov/ AppropriationsStatusTable/Index.

Table 7. Alignment of Agency R&D Funding and Regular Appropriations Bills

Department/Agency	Regular Appropriations Bill
Department of Defense	Department of Defense Appropriations Act
Department of Health and Human Services - National Institutes of Health	(1) Departments of Labor, Health and Human Services, and Education, and Related Agencies Appropriations Act (2) Department of the Interior, Environment, and Related Agencies Appropriations Act
Department of Energy	Energy and Water Development and Related Agencies Appropriations Act
National Aeronautics and Space Administration	Commerce, Justice, Science, and Related Agencies Appropriations Act
National Science Foundation	Commerce, Justice, Science, and Related Agencies Appropriations Act
Department of Agriculture	Agriculture, Rural Development, Food and Drug Administration, and Related Agencies Appropriations Act
Department of Commerce - National Institute of Standards and Technology - National Oceanic and Atmospheric Administration	Commerce, Justice, Science, and Related Agencies Appropriations Act
Department of Veterans Affairs	Military Construction and Veterans Affairs, and Related Agencies Appropriations Act
Department of the Interior	Department of the Interior, Environment, and Related Agencies Appropriations Act
Department of Transportation	Transportation, Housing and Urban Development, and Related Agencies Appropriations Act
Department of Homeland Security	Department of Homeland Security Appropriations Act
Environmental Protection Agency	Department of the Interior, Environment, and Related Agencies Appropriations Act

Source: CRS Report R40858, *Locate an Agency or Program Within Appropriations Bills*, by Justin Murray.

Department of Defense[22]

The mission of the Department of Defense is to provide "the military forces needed to deter war and ensure our nation's security."[23] Congress supports research and development activities at DOD primarily through the department's Research, Development, Test, and Evaluation (RDT&E) funding. These funds support the development of the nation's future military hardware and software and the science and technology base upon which those products rely.

Most of what DOD spends on RDT&E is appropriated in Title IV of the annual defense appropriations bill. (See **Table 8**.) However, RDT&E funds are also appropriated in other parts of the bill. For example, RDT&E funds are appropriated as part of the Defense Health Program, the Chemical Agents and Munitions Destruction Program, and the National Defense Sealift Fund. The Defense Health Program (DHP) supports the delivery of health care to DOD personnel and their families. DHP funds (including the RDT&E funds) are requested through the Defense-wide Operations and Maintenance appropriations request. The program's RDT&E funds support congressionally directed research on breast, prostate, and ovarian cancer; traumatic brain injuries; orthotics and prosthetics; and other medical conditions. Congress appropriates funds for this program in Title VI (Other Department of Defense Programs) of the defense appropriations bill. The Chemical Agents and Munitions Destruction Program supports activities to destroy the U.S. inventory of lethal chemical agents and munitions to avoid future risks and costs associated with storage. Funds for this program are requested through the Defense-wide Procurement appropriations request. Congress appropriates funds for this program also in Title VI. The National Defense Sealift Fund supports the procurement, operation and maintenance, and research and development associated with the nation's naval reserve fleet and supports a U.S. flagged merchant fleet that can serve in time of need. In some fiscal years, RDT&E funding for this effort has been requested in the Navy's Procurement request and appropriated in Title V (Revolving and Management Funds) of appropriations bills.

RDT&E funds also have been requested and appropriated as part of DOD's separate funding to support efforts in what the George W. Bush Administration termed the Global War on Terror (GWOT) and what the Obama and Trump Administrations have referred to as Overseas Contingency Operations (OCO). In appropriations bills, the term Overseas Contingency Operations/Global War on Terror (OCO/GWOT) has been used; President Trump's FY2020 budget used the term Overseas Contingency Operations. Typically, RDT&E funds for OCO activities are appropriated in Title IX and support specified Program Elements (PEs) in Title IV.

According to the Comptroller of the Department of Defense, the FY2020 OCO request is divided into three requirement categories—direct war, enduring, and OCO for base.[24] For purposes of this report, these categories of OCO funding requests are reported collectively.

---

[22] This section was written by John F. Sargent Jr., Specialist in Science and Technology Policy, CRS Resources, Science, and Industry Division.

[23] Department of Defense, https://www.defense.gov/Our-Story/.

[24] "Direct War Requirements" reflect combat or combat support costs that are not expected to continue once combat operations end at major contingency locations. "OCO for Enduring Requirements" reflects enduring in-theater and CONUS costs that will remain after combat operations end. "OCO for Base Requirements" reflects funding for base budget requirements, which support the National Defense Strategy, such as defense readiness, readiness enablers, and munitions, financed in the OCO budget to comply with the base budget defense caps included in current law. Department of Defense, Office of the Under Secretary of Defense (Comptroller)/Chief Financial Officer, *Defense Budget Overview: Department of Defense Fiscal Year 2020 Budget Request*, March 19, 2019, https://comptroller.defense.gov/Portals/45/Documents/defbudget/fy2020/ fy2020_Budget_Request_Overview_Book.pdf.

In addition, OCO/GWOT-related requests/appropriations have included money for a number of transfer funds. In the past, these have included the Iraqi Freedom Fund (IFF), the Iraqi Security Forces Fund, the Afghanistan Security Forces Fund, the Pakistan Counterinsurgency Capability Fund, and the Counter-ISIS Train and Equip Fund. Congress typically has made a single appropriation into each such fund and authorized the Secretary to make transfers to other accounts, including RDT&E, at his discretion. These transfers are eventually reflected in Title IV prior-year funding figures.

Table 8 provides the FY2019 enacted, and FY2020 request, House, Senate, and final appropriations levels for Defense RDT&E.

For FY2020, the Trump Administration requested $104.294 billion for DOD's RDT&E PEs in Title IV base funding and Title IX OCO funding, $8.334 billion (8.7%) above the enacted FY2019 level. In addition, the request included $732.3 million in RDT&E through the Defense Health Program (DHP; down $1.447 billion, 66.4% from FY2019), $875.9 million in RDT&E through the Chemical Agents and Munitions Destruction program (down $10.8 million, 1.2% from FY2019), and $3.0 million for the Inspector General for RDT&E-related activities (down $1.0 million, 25.4% from FY2019). The FY2020 budget included no RDT&E funding via the National Defense Sealift Fund, the same as the FY2019 enacted level; in some previous years RDT&E has been requested as part of this fund.

On June 19, 2019, the House-passed the Labor, Health and Human Services, Education, Defense, State, Foreign Operations, and Energy and Water Development Appropriations Act, 2020 (H.R. 2740), an omnibus appropriations measure that incorporates the Department of Defense Appropriations Act, 2020, as Division C of the bill. The House-passed bill, including both base and OCO funding would have provided:

- $101.327 billion for Title IV RDT&E PEs, $5.367 billion (5.6%) above the FY2019 enacted level and $2.967 billion (2.8%) below the request;

- $1.686 billion for the Defense Health Program, $493.3 million (22.6%) below the FY2019 enacted level, and $954.0 million (130.3%) above the request;

- $875.9 million for the Chemical Agents and Munitions Destruction program, down $10.8 million (1.2%) from the FY2019 enacted level, and equal to the request;

- $3.0 million for the Inspector General, down $1.0 million (25.0%) from the FY2019 enacted level and equal to the request; and

- no RDT&E funding for the National Defense Sealift Fund, equal to the FY2019 level and the request.

Total DOD RDT&E funding in the House-passed bill was $103.892 billion, up $4.862 billion (4.9%) from the FY2019 enacted level and down $2.013 billion (1.9%) from the request.

Congress completed action on FY2020 appropriations with passage of two consolidated appropriations acts on December 19, 2019: the Consolidated Appropriations Act, 2020 (P.L. 116-93) and the Further Consolidated Appropriations Act, 2020 (P.L. 116-94). These two acts together incorporated the 12 regular appropriations acts.

P.L. 116-93 included, as Division A, the Department of Defense Appropriations Act, 2020. RDT&E funding provided in the act, including both base and OCO funding, included:

- $105.266 billion for Title IV RDT&E PEs, $9.305 billion (9.7%) above the FY2019 enacted level and $971.2 million (0.9%) above the request;

- $2.306 billion for the Defense Health Program, $126.5 million (5.8%) above the FY2019 enacted level, and $1.574 billion (214.9%) above the request;

- $875.9 million for the Chemical Agents and Munitions Destruction program, down $10.8 million (1.2%) from the FY2019 enacted level, and equal to the request;

- $3.0 million for the Inspector General, down $1.0 million (25.0%) from the FY2019 enacted level and equal to the request; and

- no RDT&E funding for the National Defense Sealift Fund, equal to the FY2019 level and the request.

RDT&E funding can be analyzed in different ways. RDT&E funding can be characterized organizationally. Each of military department requests and receives its own RDT&E funding. So, too, do various DOD agencies (e.g., the Missile Defense Agency and the Defense Advanced Research Projects Agency), collectively aggregated within the Defense-Wide account. RDT&E funding also can be characterized by budget activity (i.e., the type of RDT&E supported). Those budget activities designated as 6.1, 6.2, and 6.3 (basic research, applied research, and advanced technology development, respectively) constitute what is called DOD's Science and Technology program (S&T) and represent the more research-oriented part of the RDT&E program. Budget activities 6.4 and 6.5 focus on the development of specific weapon systems or components for which an operational need has been determined and an acquisition program established. Budget activity 6.6 provides management support, including support for test and evaluation facilities. Budget activity 6.7 supports the development of system improvements in existing operational systems.[25]

Many congressional policymakers are particularly interested in DOD S&T program funding since these funds support the development of new technologies and the underlying science. Some in the defense community see ensuring adequate support for S&T activities as imperative to maintaining U.S. military superiority into the future. The knowledge generated at this stage of development may also contribute to advances in commercial technologies. The FY2020 request for S&T funding (base plus OCO) is $14.135 billion, $1.524 billion (9.7%) below the FY2019 enacted level. The enacted FY2020 appropriations level for S&T is $16.150 billion, $491.1million (3.1%) above the FY2019 level and $2.015 billion (14.3%) above the FY2020 request.

Within the S&T program, basic research (6.1) receives special attention, particularly by the nation's universities. DOD is not a large supporter of basic research when compared to NIH or NSF. However, over half of DOD's basic research budget is spent at universities. The Trump Administration requested $2.320 billion for DOD basic research for FY2020, $208.4 million (8.2%) below the FY2019 enacted level. The enacted FY2020 appropriations level for basic research is $2.603 billion, $74.9 million (3.0%) above the FY2019 level and $283.3 million (12.2%) above the FY2020 request. DOD is a substantial source of federal funds for university R&D in certain fields, such as aerospace, aeronautical, and astronautical engineering (40%); electrical, electronic, and communications engineering (39%); mechanical engineering (28%); computer and information sciences (28%); and materials science (25%).[26]

The House-passed bill did not provide the detail needed to assess RDT&E funding by budget activity or to compare it to FY2019 enacted levels or FY2020 request levels by budget activity.

---

[25] For additional information on the structure of Defense RDT&E, see CRS Report R44711, *Department of Defense Research, Development, Test, and Evaluation (RDT&E): Appropriations Structure*, by John F. Sargent Jr.

[26] CRS analysis of data from NSF, *Higher Education Research and Development Survey, Fiscal Year 2017,* data tables, November 20, 2018, https://ncsesdata.nsf.gov/herd/2017/.

Table 8. Department of Defense RDT&E

(total obligational authority,[a] in millions of dollars)

Budget Account	FY2019 Enacted Base + OCO	FY2020 Request Base	FY2020 Request OCO	FY2020 Request Total	FY2020 House Base	FY2020 House OCO	FY2020 House Total	FY2020 Senate Base	FY2020 Senate OCO	FY2020 Senate Total	FY2020 Enacted Base	FY2020 Enacted OCO	FY2020 Enacted Total
Army	11,375.2	12,192.8	204.1	12,396.9	12,066.1	169.1	12,235.2	n/a	n/a	n/a	12,543.4	147.3	12,690.7
Navy	18,657.8	20,270.5	164.4	20,434.9	19,163.9	164.4	19,328.4	n/a	n/a	n/a	20,155.1	164.4	20,319.5
Air Force	41,488.6	45,616.1	450.2	46,066.4	44,559.3	128.2	44,687.5	n/a	n/a	n/a	45,567.0	128.2	45,695.2
Defense-wide	24,062.0	24,347.0	828.0	25,174.9	24,472.5	382.6	24,855.1	n/a	n/a	n/a	25,938.0	394.3	26,332.3
Director, Operational Test and Evaluation	377.0	221.2	0.0	221.2	221.2	0.0	221.2	n/a	n/a	n/a	227.7	0.0	227.7
Total Title IV—By Account	**95,960.6**	**102,647.5**	**1,646.7**	**104,294.3**	**100,482.9**	**844.4**	**101,327.3**	n/a	n/a	n/a	**104,431.2**	**834.2**	**105,265.5**
Budget Activity								n/a	n/a	n/a			
6.1 Basic Research	2,528.4	2,320.0	0.0	2,320.0	n/a	n/a	n/a	n/a	n/a	n/a	2,603.3	0.0	2,603.3
6.2 Applied Research	6,025.1	5,315.5	1.7	5,317.2	n/a	n/a	n/a	n/a	n/a	n/a	6,069.8	1.7	6071.4
6.3 Advanced Technology Development	7,105.6	6,423.0	74.8	6,497.8	n/a	n/a	n/a	n/a	n/a	n/a	7,400.8	74.8	7,475.5
6.4 Advanced Component Development and Prototypes	22,005.0	26,722.2	215.0	26,937.2	n/a	n/a	n/a	n/a	n/a	n/a	26,640.0	209.0	26,849.1
6.5 Systems Dev. and Demonstration	15,577.2	17,652.3	113.0	17765.3	n/a	n/a	n/a	n/a	n/a	n/a	16,707.0	101.3	16,808.2
6.6 Management Support[b]	7,152.0	6,769.5	1.9	6,771.4	n/a	n/a	n/a	n/a	n/a	n/a	7,058.8	209.1	7,267.9
6.7 Operational Systems Development[c]	35,567.2	37,445.0	1,240.3	38,685.3	n/a	n/a	n/a	n/a	n/a	n/a	37,951.5	238.4	38,189.9
Total Title IV—by Budget Activity	**95,960.6**	**102,647.5**	**1,646.7**	**104,294.3**	**100,482.9**	**844.4**	**101,327.3**	n/a	n/a	n/a	**104,431.2**	**834.2**	**105,265.5**

Budget Account	FY2019 Enacted	FY2020 Request			FY2020 House			FY2020 Senate			FY2020 Enacted		
	Base + OCO	Base	OCO	Total	Base	OCO	Total	Base	OCO	Total	Base	OCO	Total
Title V—Revolving and Management Funds								n/a	n/a	n/a			
National Defense Sealift Fund	0.0	0.0	0.0	0.0	0.0	0.0	0.0	n/a	n/a	n/a	0.0	0.0	0.0
Title VI—Other Defense Programs								n/a	n/a	n/a			
Defense Health Program	2,179.6	732.3	0.0	732.3	1,686.3	0.0	1,686.3	n/a	n/a	n/a	2,306.1	0.0	2,306.1
Chemical Agents and Munitions Destruction	886.7	875.9	0.0	875.9	875.9	0.0	875.9	n/a	n/a	n/a	875.9	0.0	875.9
Inspector General	4.0	3.0	0.0	3.0	3.0	0.0	3.0	n/a	n/a	n/a	3.0	0.0	3.0
Grand Total	99,030.9	104,258.7	1,646.7	105,905.4	103,048.1	844.4	103,892.5	n/a	n/a	n/a	107,616.2	834.2	108,450.4

Source: CRS analysis of *Department of Defense Budget, Fiscal Year 2020, RDT&E Programs (R-1)*, March 2019; H.R. 2740 (as passed by the House), and H.R. 1158.

Notes: Totals may differ from the sum of the components due to rounding. "FY2020 Senate" is not available (n/a); the Senate did not take action on a separate measure related to funding for DOD.

a. According to DOD, "Total Obligation Authority (TOA) is the sum of (1) all budget authority (BA) granted (or requested) from the Congress in a given year, (2) amounts authorized to be credited to a specific fund, (3) BA transferred from another appropriation, and (4) Unobligated balances of BA from previous years which remain available for obligation. In practice, this term is used primarily in discussing the DOD budget, and most often refers to TOA as the 'direct program,' which equates to only (1) and (2) above." DOD defines "budget authority" as "the authority becoming available during the year to enter into obligations that result in immediate or future outlays of Government funds." See DOD 7000.14-R, "Department of Defense Financial Management Regulation," http://comptroller.defense.gov/fmr.aspx.

b. Includes funding for Director of Test and Evaluation.

c. Includes funding for Classified Programs.

Department of Health and Human Services

The mission of the Department of Health and Human Services (HHS) is "to enhance and protect the health and well-being of all Americans ... by providing for effective health and human services and fostering advances in medicine, public health, and social services."[27] This section focuses on HHS research and development funded through the National Institutes of Health (NIH), an HHS agency that accounts for nearly 97% of total HHS R&D funding.[28] Other HHS agencies that provide funding for R&D include the Centers for Disease Control and Prevention (CDC), Centers for Medicare and Medicaid Services (CMS), Food and Drug Administration (FDA), Agency for Healthcare Research and Quality (AHRQ), Health Resources and Services Administration (HRSA), and Administration for Children and Families (ACF); additional R&D funding is attributed to departmental management.[29]

National Institutes of Health[30]

NIH is the primary agency of the federal government charged with performing and supporting biomedical and behavioral research. It also has major roles in training biomedical researchers and disseminating health information. The NIH mission is "to seek fundamental knowledge about the nature and behavior of living systems and the application of that knowledge to enhance health, lengthen life, and reduce illness and disability."[31] The agency consists of the NIH Office of the Director (OD) and 27 institutes and centers (ICs).

The OD sets overall policy for NIH and coordinates the programs and activities of all NIH components, particularly in areas of research that involve multiple institutes. The ICs focus on particular diseases (e.g., National Cancer Institute), areas of human health and development (e.g., National Institute on Aging), or scientific research fields or support (e.g., National Center for Advancing Translational Sciences). Each IC plans and manages its own research programs in coordination with OD. As shown in **Table 9**, separate appropriations are provided to 24 of the 27 ICs, as well as to OD, the Innovation Account (established by the 21st Century Cures Act, P.L. 114-255), and an intramural Buildings and Facilities account. The other three centers, which perform centralized support services, are funded through transfers from the other ICs.

NIH supports and conducts a wide range of basic and clinical research, research training, and health information dissemination across all fields of biomedical and behavioral sciences. According to NIH, about 10% of the NIH budget supports intramural research projects conducted by the nearly 6,000 NIH federal scientists, most of whom are located on the NIH campus in Bethesda, MD. More than 80% of NIH's budget goes to the extramural research community in the form of grants, contracts, and other awards. This funding supports research performed by

---

[27] U.S. Department of Health and Human Services, "About," http://www.hhs.gov/about.

[28] CRS analysis of data from OMB, *Analytical Perspectives, Budget of the United States Government, Fiscal Year 2020,* 2019, p. 268, https://www.whitehouse.gov/wp-content/uploads/2019/03/spec-fy2020.pdf.

[29] Ibid.

[30] This section was written by Kavya Sekar, Analyst in Health Policy, CRS Domestic Social Policy Division. For background information on NIH, see CRS Report R41705, *The National Institutes of Health (NIH): Background and Congressional Issues,* by Judith A. Johnson and Kavya Sekar.

[31] HHS, National Institutes of Health, "About NIH, What We Do, Mission and Goals," http://www.nih.gov/about-nih/what-we-do/mission-goals.

more than 300,000 nonfederal scientists and technical personnel who work at more than 2,500 universities, hospitals, medical schools, and other research institutions.[32]

Funding for NIH comes primarily from the annual Labor, HHS, and Education (LHHS) appropriations act, with an additional amount for Superfund-related activities from the Interior/Environment appropriations act. Those two appropriations acts provide NIH's discretionary budget authority. In addition, NIH has receives mandatory funding of $150 million annually provided in the Public Health Service Act (PHSA), Section 330B, for a special program on type 1 diabetes research. Under current law, no new funding will be available for this program after September 30, 2019.[33]

Some funding is also pursuant to the "PHS Evaluation Tap" transfer authority, under Section 241 of the PHS Act (42 U.S.C. §238j). This provision allows the Secretary of HHS, with the approval of appropriators, to redistribute a portion of eligible PHS agency appropriations across HHS for program evaluation purposes.[34] Although the PHS Act limits the tap to no more than 1% of eligible appropriations, in recent years annual LHHS appropriations acts have specified a higher amount (2.5% in FY2019, P.L. 115-245)[35] and have also typically directed specific amounts of funding from the tap for transfer to a number of HHS programs. The assessment has the effect of redistributing appropriated funds for specific purposes among PHS and other HHS agencies. NIH, with the largest budget among the PHS agencies, has historically been the largest "donor" of program evaluation funds; until recently, it had been a relatively minor recipient.[36] Provisions in recent LHHS appropriations acts have directed specific tap transfers to NIH, making NIH a net recipient of tap funds.

President Trump's FY2020 budget request proposes for NIH a total program level of $34.368 billion, a decrease of $4.941 billion (12.6%) compared with FY2019 enacted levels.[37] The proposed FY2020 program level total would include

- $33.410 billion provided through LHHS appropriations (including the full amount authorized by the 21st Century Cures Act);

- $741 million pursuant to the PHS evaluation transfer;

- $66.581 million provided through Interior/Environment appropriations for Superfund-related activities; and

- $150 million in proposed funding for the mandatory type 1 diabetes program, authorized by PHSA Sec. 330B. For this proposal, Congress and the President would need to enact legislation to extend the special diabetes program funding,

---

[32] NIH, "What We Do: Budget," https://www.nih.gov/about-nih/what-we-do/budget.

[33] 42 U.S.C. §254c-2.

[34] For more information on the PHS evaluation tap, or PHS Evaluation Set-Aside, see discussion in CRS Report R44916, *Public Health Service Agencies: Overview and Funding (FY2016-FY2018)*, coordinated by C. Stephen Redhead and Agata Dabrowska.

[35] H.R. 6157, p. 109.

[36] For more information, see the "PHS Evaluation Set-Aside" section of CRS Report R44916, *Public Health Service Agencies: Overview and Funding (FY2016-FY2018)*. By convention, budget tables such as **Table 9** do not subtract the amount of the evaluation tap from the donor agencies' appropriations.

[37] Based on CRS analysis using budget data from NIH, "FY2020 Justification of Estimates for Appropriations Committees—Overview, Vol. 1," p. 78, and the National Institute of Environmental Health Sciences appropriation from the Consolidated Appropriations Act, 2019 (P.L. 116-6).

because under current law, no new funding will be available for this program after September 30, 2019.[38]

Under the FY2020 budget proposal, all existing ICs and budget activity lines, except for Buildings and Facilities, would receive a decrease compared to FY2019 enacted levels (see **Table 9**).[39] The Buildings and Facilities appropriation of $200 million would not change from FY2019 to FY2020.

Additionally, the FY2020 Budget Request proposes consolidating the Agency for Healthcare Research and Quality into NIH, forming a 28th IC—the National Institute for Research on Safety and Quality (NIRSQ). The creation of a new NIH institute would require an amendment to PHSA Section 401(d), which specifies that "[i]n the National Institutes of Health, the number of national research institutes and national centers may not exceed a total of 27." Under the request, NISRQ would receive $256 million in funding for FY2020.[40]

The main funding mechanism NIH uses to support extramural research is research project grants (RPGs), which are competitive, peer-reviewed, and largely investigator-initiated. Historically, over 50% of the NIH budget is used to support RPGs, which include salaries for investigators and research staff.[41] The FY2020 budget proposes to reduce the average cost of RPGs by capping the percentage of an investigator's salary that can be paid with grant funds to 90%.[42]

The FY2020 NIH budget request also includes $492 million made available through the 21st Century Cures Act (see text box below; hereinafter referred to as "The Cures Act"). The Cures Act (P.L. 114-255) specifies that $149 million is for the Precision Medicine Initiative, $140 million is for the BRAIN Initiative, $195 million is for cancer research, and $8 million is for research on regenerative medicine for FY2020.[43]

In June 2019, the House passed two consolidated appropriations bills with proposed funding levels for NIH accounts: H.R. 2740 with proposed LHHS appropriations[44] and H.R. 3055 with proposed Interior/Environment appropriations.[45] In summary, House-passed legislation would provide NIH FY2020 funding levels made up of

---

[38] 42 U.S.C. §254c-2.

[39] Though the budget request provides an increase to the National Institute of General Medical Sciences through discretionary LHHS budget authority, the total amount for NIGMS with the PHS evaluation transfer included is less than FY2019 enacted levels. For proposed FY2020 IC funding levels see NIH, "FY2020 Justification of Estimates for Appropriations Committees—Overview, Vol. 1," p. 78.

[40] The FY2020 request for NISRQ is roughly $82 million less than the discretionary amount appropriated to Agency for Healthcare Research and Quality (AHRQ) in FY2019. In addition, AHRQ also received roughly $112.5 million in mandatory funds in FY2019 from the Patient-Centered Outcomes Research Trust Fund (PCORTF). Funding for the PCORTF is scheduled to expire at the end of FY2019. The FY2020 President's budget does not request any new mandatory funds for the PCORTF. For more information, see "FY2020 Justification of Estimates for Appropriations Committees—NIH National Institute for Research on Safety and Quality," p. 6.

[41] CRS analysis of data from NIH, *Actual Total Obligations by Budget Mechanism: FY2000-FY2018*, March 18, 2019, https://officeofbudget.od.nih.gov/pdfs/FY20/Mechanism-Detail-for-NIH-FY-2000-FY-2018.pdf.

[42] NIH, "FY2020 Justification of Estimates for Appropriations Committees—Overview, Vol. 1," p. 13.

[43] P.L. 114-255, Sec. 1001(b)(4).

[44] The Labor, Health and Human Services, Education, Defense, State, Foreign Operations, and Energy and Water Development Appropriations Act, 2020.

[45] Commerce, Justice, Science, Agriculture, Rural Development, Food and Drug Administration, Interior, Environment, Military Construction, Veterans Affairs, Transportation, and Housing and Urban Development Appropriations Act, 2020.

- $39.937 billion provided through LHHS appropriations (including the full amount authorized by the 21st Century Cures Act);

- $1.146 billion pursuant to the PHS evaluation transfer directed in the LHHS appropriations bill; and

- $80 million provided through Interior/Environment appropriations for Superfund-related activities;

In total, the House legislation discussed above would provide NIH discretionary BA and PHS evaluation tap funding of $41.2 billion—$2.0 billion (+5.1%) more than FY2019 enacted levels and $6.9 billion (+20.3%) more than proposed by the Administration's FY2020 budget request. The House appropriations bills would provide an increase to all IC accounts compared to FY2019 enacted levels, except for Buildings and Facilities which would be provided the same funding level as FY2019 of $200 million.

Legislation to extend the mandatory funding for the Special Diabetes Program for type 1 diabetes research has received committee consideration in the House, the Special Diabetes Program Reauthorization Act of 2019 (H.R. 2668). The bill would extend the program through FY2024 and increase annual funding by $50 million compared to current law—from $150 million to $200 million. If passed by the House, the total House-proposed FY2020 NIH program level would be $41.4 billion.

The House did not adopt the Administration's proposal to consolidate the Agency for Healthcare Research and Quality into NIH nor to cap the percentage of an investigator's salary that can be paid with grant funds to 90%. The report accompanying the LHHS appropriations bill (H.Rept. 116-62) did not address either of these proposals.[46]

The Senate has not begun consideration of FY2020 appropriations. However, legislation to extend mandatory funding for type 1 diabetes research has been introduced by the chair of Senate Health, Labor, Education, and Pensions (HELP) committee, Senator Alexander. The Community and Public Health Programs Extension Act (S. 192) would extend the Special Diabetes Program for type 1 diabetes through FY2024 with the same annual funding level provided under current law—$150 million.

---

[46] U.S. Congress, House Committee on Appropriations, Subcommittee on the Departments of Labor, Health and Human Services, Education, and Related Agencies, *Department of Labor, Health and Human Services, and Education, and Related Agencies Appropriations Bill, 2020*, Report to accompany H.R. 2740, 116th Cong., 1st sess., May 15, 2016, H.Rept. 116-92 (Washington: GPO, 2019).

The 21ˢᵗ Century Cures Act and the NIH Innovation Account

The 21st Century Cures Act (P.L. 114-255) created the NIH Innovation account and specified that funds in the account must be appropriated in order to be available for expenditure. The Cures Act specified that the following amounts shall be transferred to the NIH Innovation account: $352 million for FY2017; $496 million for FY2018; $711 million for FY2019; $492 million for FY2020; $404 million for FY2021; $496 million for FY2022; $1,085 million for FY2023; $407 million for FY2024; $127 million for FY2025; and $226 million for FY2026.

The Cures Act authorizes four projects (with total funding from FY2017 to FY2026): the Precision Medicine Initiative ($1.455 billion), the BRAIN Initiative ($1.511 billion), cancer research ($1.8 billion), and regenerative medicine using adult stem cells ($30 million). Amounts, once appropriated, are to be available until expended. The NIH Director may transfer these amounts from the NIH Innovation account to other NIH accounts but only for the purposes specified in the Cures Act. If the NIH Director determines that the funds for any of the four Innovation Projects are not necessary, the amounts may be transferred back to the NIH Innovation account. This transfer authority is in addition to other transfer authorities provided by law.

For further information, see CRS Report R44720, *The 21st Century Cures Act (Division A of P.L. 114-255)*, and CRS Report R44723, *Overview of Further Continuing Appropriations for FY2017 (H.R. 2028)*.

The President's FY2020 budget identifies several research priorities for NIH in the coming year. The overview below outlines some of these priority themes in the budget request. Selected responses from congressional report language are also provided.

1. Confronting the Opioids Crisis

The request includes $1.3 billion designated for opioids and pain research across NIH, with $500 million of the total for the Helping to End Addiction Long-Term (HEAL) initiative. The HEAL Initiative, launched in April 2018, aims to accelerate the development of new medications and devices to treat opioid addiction. In addition, NIH plans to support research on neonatal abstinence syndrome, chronic pain, and other opioids-related issues.[47]

The House also recommends no less than $500 million for the HEAL Initiative provided equally ($250 million each) through appropriations to the National Institute of Neurological Disorders and Stroke (NINDS) and the National Institute on Drug Abuse (NIDA).[48]

2. Pediatric Research

The FY2020 request proposes $50 million in designated funding for a pediatric cancer initiative. The initiative, designed to complement existing pediatric cancer research, would aggregate data on pediatric cancer cases and coordinate existing datasets to create a "comprehensive, shared resource to support research on childhood cancer in all its forms."[49] The request also designates $15 million for the Institutional Development Award (IDeA) States Pediatric Clinical Trials Network to support pediatric clinical studies, such as on the "dosing, safety, and efficacy of drugs that are commonly prescribed to children."[50]

House FY2020 appropriations would include the $50 million in designated funding for a pediatric cancer initiative, and the report includes additional language to prioritize research on brain cancer

---

[47] HHS, "Budget in Brief—FY2020," pp. 53-54, https://www.hhs.gov/sites/default/files/fy-20 20-budget-in-brief.pdf.

[48] H.Rept. 116-62, pp. 90-101.

[49] HHS, "Budget in Brief—FY2020," p. 55, https://www.hhs.gov/sites/default/files/fy-2020-budget-in-brief.pdf.

[50] Ibid., p. 56. The Institutional Development Award (IDeA) program is designed to build research capacity in states that have had historically low levels of NIH funding. Currently, 23 states and Puerto Rico are eligible for IDeA funding. See National Institute of General Medical Sciences (NIGMS), "Institutional Development Award," https://www.nigms.nih.gov/Research/DRCB/IDeA/Pages/default.aspx, and CRS Report R44689, *Established Program to Stimulate Competitive Research (EPSCoR): Background and Selected Issues*, by Laurie A. Harris.

in children, to continue the work of the Children's Oncology Group, and for NIH to collaborate with pediatric immunotherapy trials.[51] The House did not designate a funding level for the Institutional Development Award (IDeA) States Pediatric Clinical Trials Network.

3. Supporting the Next Generation of Researchers

The request would provide $100 million in dedicated funding for the Next Generation Researchers Initiative, which aims to support new and early stage scientists in attaining their first NIH grants.[52] Through the program, NIH ICs are to create funding pathways and other strategies targeted at new and early-stage scientists, and would be required to collect data and evaluate their outcomes.[53]

The House report stated that their proposed funding increases provided to all IC accounts, in part, would allow for "an increase in the number of new and competing Research Project Grants, with a focus on early-stage investigators and investigators seeking first-time renewals."[54]

4. Ending the HIV Epidemic

As a part of a proposed HHS wide plan, "Ending the HIV Epidemic: A Plan for America," the FY2020 request designates $6 million in funding to Centers for AIDS Research to collect data and inform HHS on best practices for the initiative. The goal for the plan is to reduce new infections by 75% in the next 5 years, and by 90% in the next 10 years.[55]

The House would provide an increase of $6 million compared to FY2019 funding for Centers for AIDS Research, raising the funding level from $45 million to $51 million.[56]

5. New Technologies and Biomedical Research

NIH plans to continue to support biomedical innovations using new technologies, including for diagnosis, monitoring, and treatment. An example includes a smartphone-based system for people with diabetes to monitor blood glucose levels. NIH also aims to accelerate scientific discovery through new data science methods. In June 2018, NIH released a Strategic Plan for Data Science, with an agency-wide plan for increasing and improving its use of large biomedical datasets. In addition, NIH plans to convene a new working group on artificial intelligence, machine learning, and biomedical research.[57] The House report did not specifically address new technologies and biomedical research.[58]

---

[51] H.Rept. 116-62. pp. 81-85.

[52] HHS, "Budget in Brief—FY2020," p. 56, https://www.hhs.gov/sites/default/files/fy-2020-budget-in-brief.pdf.

[53] NIH, "Next Generation Researchers Initiative," https://grants.nih.gov/ngri.htm.

[54] H.Rept. 116-62, p. 81.

[55] Ibid., p. 56.

[56] H.Rept. 116-62, p. 92.

[57] Ibid., p. 57, https://www.hhs.gov/sites/default/files/fy-2020-budget-in-brief.pdf.

[58] H.Rept. 116-62.

Table 9. National Institutes of Health Funding

(budget authority, in millions of dollars)

Institutes/Centers	FY2019 Enacted	FY2020 Request	FY2020 House	FY2020 Senate	FY2020 Enacted
Cancer Institute (NCI)	$6,144	$5,247	$6,444		
Heart, Lung, and Blood Institute (NHLBI)	$3,488	$3,003	$3,659		
Dental/Craniofacial Research (NIDCR)	$462	$397	$484		
Diabetes/Digestive/Kidney (NIDDK)[a]	$2,030	$1,747	$2,129		
Neurological Disorders/Stroke (NINDS)	$2,274	$2,026	$2,386		
Allergy/Infectious Diseases (NIAID)	$5,523	$4,754	$5,808		
General Medical Sciences (NIGMS)[b]	$1,726	$1,732	$1,886		
Child Health/Human Development (NICHD)	$1,506	$1,297	$1,580		
National Eye Institute (NEI)	$797	$686	$835		
Environmental Health Sciences (NIEHS)[c]	$775	$667	$813		
National Institute on Aging (NIA)	$3,083	$2,654	$3,286		
Arthritis/Musculoskeletal/Skin Diseases (NIAMS)	$605	$521	$635		
Deafness/Communication Disorders (NIDCD)	$474	$408	$498		
National Institute of Mental Health (NIMH)	$1,870	$1,630	$1,962		
National Institute on Drug Abuse (NIDA)	$1,420	$1,296	$1,489		
Alcohol Abuse/Alcoholism (NIAAA)	$526	$452	$551		
Nursing Research (NINR)	$163	$140	$171		
Human Genome Research Institute (NHGRI)	$576	$495	$604		
Biomedical Imaging/Bioengineering (NIBIB)	$389	$336	$408		
Minority Health/Health Disparities (NIMHD)	$315	$271	$341		
Complementary/Integrative Health (NCCIH)	$146	$126	$154		
Advancing Translational Sciences (NCATS)	$806	$694	$846		
Fogarty International Center (FIC)	$78	$67	$85		
National Library of Medicine (NLM)	$442	$380	$464		
Office of Director (OD)[d]	$1,917	$1,769	$2,063		
Innovation Account[e]	$196	$157	$157		
Buildings and Facilities (B&F)	$200	$200	$200		
National Institute for Research on Safety & Quality (NIRSQ)[f]	—	$256	—		
Subtotal, NIH (LHHS Discretionary BA)	**$37,933**	**$33,411**	**$39,937**		
PHS Program Evaluation (provided to NIGMS)	$1,147	$741	$1,147		
Superfund (Interior approp. to NIEHS)[g]	$79	$67	$80		
Mandatory type 1 diabetes funds[h]	$150	$150	$200		
NIH Program Level	**$39,308**	**$34,368**	**$41,364**		

Sources: NIH, "FY2020 Justification of Estimates for Appropriations Committees-Vol 1, Overview," p. 78, and H.Rept. 116-62, pp. 332-334, except as noted below.

Notes: Totals may differ from the sum of the components due to rounding. Amounts in table may differ from actuals in many cases. By convention, budget tables such as **Table 9** do not subtract the amount of transfers to the evaluation tap from the agencies' appropriation. Figures for the columns headed "FY2020 Senate," and "FY2020 Enacted" will be added, if available, as each action is completed.

a.   Amounts for the National Institute of Diabetes and Digestive and Kidney Diseases (NIDDK) do not include mandatory funding for type 1 diabetes research (see note h).

b.   Amounts for National Institute of General Medical Sciences (NIGMS) do not include funds from PHS Evaluation Set-Aside (§241 of the PHS Act). Though the budget request provides an increase to NIGMS through discretionary LHHS budget authority compared to FY2019, the total amount for NIGMS with the PHS evaluation transfer included is less than FY2019 enacted levels.

c.   Amounts for National Institute of Environmental Health Sciences (NIEHS) do not include Interior/Environment Appropriations amount for Superfund research (see note g).

d.   Includes $12.6 million for the Gabriella Miller Kids First Research Act.

e.   The amount shown for the NIH Innovation Account in each column represents only a portion ($196 million for FY2019, $157 million for the FY2020 request) of the total appropriation to the account ($711 million for FY2020, $492 million for the FY2020 request). The remaining funds for this account are incorporated, where applicable, into the totals for other ICs. For the FY2020 request, this includes $195 to NCI for cancer research and $70 million to each of NINDS and NIMH for the BRAIN Initiative.

f.   Amount for NIRSQ does not include the estimated $112.5 million in mandatory funding transfers from the Patient-Centered Outcomes Research Trust Fund (PCORTF) in FY2019, which were provided outside of the annual appropriations process. Mandatory funding for the PCORTF is scheduled to expire at the end of FY2019. The President's FY2020 budget did not request any new funding for the PCORTF.

g.   This is a separate account in the Interior/Environment appropriations for National Institute of Environmental Health Sciences (NIEHS) research activities related to Superfund. The FY2019 enacted amount is from Title III from the Consolidated Appropriations Act, 2019 (P.L. 116-6), and the House proposed FY2020 amount is from House-passed Department of the Interior, Environment, and Related Agencies Appropriations Act, 2020 (H.R. 3055).

h.   Mandatory funds are available to NIDDK for type 1 diabetes research under PHSA Sec. 330B (provided by §50902 P.L. 115-123 for FY2018 and FY2019). These funds are specified at $150 million annually. Under current law, no new funds will be available after September 30, 2019. The FY2020 request represents proposed funding to be extended at current law levels. The House-proposed amount is based on H.R. 2668, introduced legislation that has received committee consideration to extend funding under Sec. 330B.

Department of Energy[59]

The Department of Energy (DOE) was established in 1977 by the Department of Energy Organization Act (P.L. 95-91), which combined energy-related programs from a variety of agencies with defense-related nuclear programs that dated back to the Manhattan Project. Today, DOE conducts basic scientific research in fields ranging from nuclear physics to the biological and environmental sciences; basic and applied R&D relating to energy production and use; and R&D on nuclear weapons, nuclear nonproliferation, and defense nuclear reactors. The department has a system of 17 national laboratories around the country, mostly operated by contractors, that together account for about 40% of all DOE expenditures.

The Administration's FY2020 budget request for DOE included about $12.283 billion for R&D and related activities, including programs in three broad categories: science, national security, and energy. This request was 21.8% less than the enacted FY2019 amount of $15.712 billion. The House bill would have provided about $16.385 billion. The Senate bill would have provided

---

[59] This section was written by Daniel Morgan, Specialist in Science and Technology Policy, CRS Resources, Science, and Industry Division.

about $17.338 billion. The enacted appropriations included about $16.982 billion. (See **Table 10** for details.)

The request for the DOE Office of Science was $5.546 billion, a decrease of 15.8% from the FY2019 appropriation of $6.585 billion. Funding was to decrease for each of the office's six major research programs. In Basic Energy Sciences, almost half the proposed decrease resulted from the approaching end of construction on the Linac Coherent Light Source II (no funding requested for FY2020, down from $129 million in FY2019). Funding for Biological and Environmental Research was to decrease by $211 million (29.9%), with reductions concentrated in the Earth and Environmental Systems Sciences subprogram. In Advanced Scientific Computing Research, the Office of Science Exascale Computing Project was to receive $189 million, down 18.9% from $233 million in FY2019.[60] Funding for Fusion Energy Sciences was to decrease by $161 million (28.6%). Within Fusion Energy Sciences, the U.S. contribution to construction of the International Thermonuclear Experimental Reactor (ITER), a fusion energy demonstration and research facility in France, was to be $107 million (down from $132 million in FY2019).

The House bill would have provided $6.870 billion for the Office of Science. All six of the major programs would have received more than the Administration's request; all except Basic Energy Sciences would have received more than they did in FY2019. In the Biological and Environmental Research program, funding for Earth and Environmental Systems Sciences would have been about $349 million, up from $337 million in FY2019 and more than double the Administration's request. In Advanced Scientific Computing Research, the Exascale Computing Project would have received the requested amount. Fusion Energy Sciences would have received 71% more than the request and 22% more than in FY2019, including $230 million for the U.S. contribution to ITER.

The Senate bill would have provided $7.215 billion for the Office of Science. All six of the major programs would have received more than the Administration's request and more than they did in FY2019. The Senate report did not specify funding for Earth and Environmental Systems Sciences, but it recommended amounts at or above the FY2019 level for several specified activities within the program. In Advanced Scientific Computing Research, the Exascale Computing Project would have received the requested amount. Fusion Energy Sciences would have received 42% more than the request and 1% more than in FY2019, including $180 million for the U.S. contribution to ITER.

The enacted appropriation for the Office of Science was $7.000 billion. All six major programs received more than the request and more than in FY2019. Funding for Earth and Environmental Systems Sciences was up to $359 million. The explanatory statement was silent regarding the Exascale Computing Project; the project was therefore funded at the requested level as recommended in the House and Senate reports. Fusion Energy Sciences received 67% more than the request and 19% more than in FY2019, including $242 million for the U.S. contribution to ITER.

The request for DOE national security R&D was $4.425 billion, an increase of 0.4% from $4.406 billion in FY2019. Funding for Weapons Activities RDT&E was to increase 13.1%, including an increase of $123 million for Advanced Simulation and Computing, an increase of $95 million (190.3%) for Enhanced Capabilities for Subcritical Experiments, and $481 million (a decrease of $64 million from $545 million in FY2019) for Inertial Confinement Fusion. In Defense Nuclear Nonproliferation R&D, reactor conversion activities in the Nonproliferation Fuels Development

---

[60] This project is part, but not all, of the DOE-wide Exascale Computing Initiative.

subprogram were to transfer to a non-R&D account; excluding this accounting change, funding for the rest of Defense Nuclear Nonproliferation R&D was to increase by 3.8%. Funding for the Naval Reactors program was to decrease by 7.8% overall, with increases for operations, infrastructure, and technology development offset by previously planned decreases in funding for construction and two major multiyear projects.

The House bill would have provided $4.460 billion for DOE national security R&D. In the Weapons Activities account, Advanced Simulation and Computing and Enhanced Capabilities for Subcritical Experiments would both have received the requested amounts, while Inertial Confinement Fusion would have received $565 million. Within Defense Nuclear Nonproliferation R&D, the bill would have provided $15 million for Nonproliferation Fuels Development to develop low-enriched fuels to replace highly enriched uranium in naval applications. The bill would have provided 1% less than the request for Naval Reactors.

The Senate bill would have provided $4.646 billion for DOE national security R&D. In the Weapons Activities account, Advanced Simulation and Computing and Enhanced Capabilities for Subcritical Experiments would both have received the requested amounts, while Inertial Confinement Fusion would have received $570 million. Within Defense Nuclear Nonproliferation R&D, the bill would have provided $15 million for Nonproliferation Fuels Development. The bill would have provided the requested amount for Naval Reactors.

The enacted appropriations included $4.609 billion for national security R&D. In the Weapons Activities account, Advanced Simulation and Computing and Enhanced Capabilities for Subcritical Experiments both received the requested amounts, while Inertial Confinement Fusion received $565 million. Within Defense Nuclear Nonproliferation R&D, Nonproliferation Fuels Development received $15 million. The enacted appropriation for Naval Reactors was the same as the request.

The request for DOE energy R&D was $2.313 billion, a decrease of 51.0% from $4.721 billion in FY2019. Many of the proposed reductions in this category were similar to the Administration's FY2019 budget proposals. Funding for energy efficiency and renewable energy R&D was to decrease by 66.3%, with reductions in all major research areas and a shift in emphasis toward early-stage R&D rather than later-stage development and deployment. Funding for fossil energy R&D was to decrease by 24.1%, with reductions focused particularly on coal carbon capture and storage ($69 million, down from $199 million in FY2019) and natural gas technologies ($11 million, down from $51 million in FY2019). The request for fuel cycle R&D was $90 million (down from $264 million in FY2019), and nuclear energy as a whole was to decrease by 37.9%, with no funding requested for the Integrated University Program ($5 million in FY2019) or the Supercritical Transformational Electric Power (STEP) R&D initiative ($5 million in FY2019). The Advanced Research Projects Agency-Energy (ARPA-E), which is intended to advance high-impact energy technologies that have too much technical and financial uncertainty to attract near-term private-sector investment, was to be terminated.

The House bill would have provided $5.055 billion for DOE energy R&D. Funding for energy efficiency and renewable energy R&D would have been more than triple the request and about 11% more than in FY2019, with increases relative to FY2019 in all major research areas. Funding for fossil energy R&D would have been about the same as in FY2019, including $227 million for coal carbon capture and storage and $48 million for natural gas R&D. Funding for nuclear energy would also have been about the same as in FY2019, including $319 million for fuel cycle R&D and $5 million each for the Integrated University Program and STEP R&D. ARPA-E would have received $428 million, an increase of 17% relative to FY2019.

The Senate bill would have provided $5.478 billion for DOE energy R&D. Funding for energy efficiency and renewable energy R&D would have been 3.5 times the request and 18% more than in FY2019, with increases relative to FY2019 in all major research areas. Funding for fossil energy R&D would have been $60 million more than in FY2019, including $216 million for coal carbon capture and storage and $55 million for natural gas R&D. Funding for nuclear energy would have been $192 million more than in FY2019, including $315 million for fuel cycle R&D and $5 million each for the Integrated University Program and STEP R&D. ARPA-E would have received $428 million.

The enacted appropriations included $5.372 billion for DOE energy R&D. Funding for energy efficiency and renewable energy R&D was between the House and Senate recommendations, with increases relative to FY2019 in all major research areas. Funding for fossil energy R&D was also between the House and Senate recommendations, including $218 million for coal carbon capture and storage and $51 million for natural gas R&D. Funding for nuclear energy was $167 million more than in FY2019, including $305 million for fuel cycle R&D and $5 million each for the Integrated University Program and STEP R&D. ARPA-E received $425 million.

Table 10. Department of Energy R&D and Related Activities

(budget authority, in millions of dollars)

	FY2019 Enacted	FY2020 Request	FY2020 House	FY2020 Senate	FY2020 Enacted
Science	**$6,585**	**$5,546**	**$6,870**	**$7,215**	**$7,000**
Basic Energy Sciences	2,166	1,858	2,143	2,325	2,213
High Energy Physics	980	768	1,045	1,065	1,045
Biological and Environmental Research	705	494	730	770	750
Nuclear Physics	690	625	735	736	713
Advanced Scientific Computing Research	936	921	957	1,029	980
Fusion Energy Sciences	564	403	688	570	671
Other	545	477	572	720	628
National Security	**4,406**	**4,425**	**4,460**	**4,646**	**4,609**
Weapons Activities RDT&E	2,014	2,278	2,283	2,442	2,398
Naval Reactors	1,789	1,648	1,629	1,648	1,648
Defense Nuclear Nonproliferation R&D	576	495	520	525	533
Defense Environmental Cleanup Technol. Devel.	28	3	28	30	30
Energy	**4,721**	**2,313**	**5,055**	**5,478**	**5,372**
Energy Efficiency and Renewable Energy[a]	2,067	696	2,296	2,442	2,419[b]
Fossil Energy R&D	740	562	739	800	750
Nuclear Energy	1,326	824	1,321	1,518	1,493
Electricity / Electricity Delivery	132	156	173	194	190
Cybersec., En. Security, & Emerg. Response R&D	90	75	98	96	95
Advanced Research Projects Agency-Energy	366	0[c]	428	428	425
DOE, Total	**15,712**	**12,283**	**16,385**	**17,338**	**16,982**

Source: FY2019 enacted from P.L. 115-244 and H.Rept. 115-929. FY2020 request from DOE FY2020 congressional budget justification, https://www.energy.gov/cfo/downloads/fy-2020-budget-justification. FY2020

House from H.R. 2740 as passed by the House and H.Rept. 116-83. FY2020 Senate from S. 2470 as reported and S.Rept. 116-102. FY2020 enacted from P.L. 116-94 and explanatory statement, *Congressional Record*, December 17, 2019, Book III.

Notes: Totals may differ from the sum of the components due to rounding.

a. Excluding Weatherization and Intergovernmental Activities.

b. Reduced for $58 million rescission of prior-year unobligated balances. Some of that rescission may ultimately be taken from non-R&D activities.

c. In addition, the request proposed to rescind $287 million in unobligated funds from prior years.

National Aeronautics and Space Administration[61]

The National Aeronautics and Space Administration (NASA) was created in 1958 by the National Aeronautics and Space Act (P.L. 85-568) to conduct civilian space and aeronautics activities. NASA has research programs in planetary science, Earth science, heliophysics, astrophysics, and aeronautics, as well as development programs for future human spacecraft and for multipurpose space technology such as advanced propulsion systems. In addition, NASA operates the International Space Station (ISS) as a facility for R&D and other purposes.

The Administration initially requested about $17.845 billion for NASA R&D in FY2020. This was 0.1% less than FY2019 funding of about $17.865 billion. A budget amendment subsequently requested an additional $1.597 billion.[62] The House bill (H.R. 3055) would have provided about $19.051 billion. The Senate bill (S. 2584, incorporated into the Senate amendment to H.R. 3055) would have provided about $19.534 billion. The enacted appropriation included about $19.439 billion. For a breakdown of these amounts, see **Table 11**. NASA R&D funding comes through five accounts: Science; Aeronautics; Space Technology (called Exploration Technology in the Administration's budget request); Exploration (Deep Space Exploration Systems in the request); and the ISS, Commercial Crew, and Commercial Low Earth Orbit (LEO) Development portions of Space Operations (called LEO and Spaceflight Operations in the request).

The initial FY2020 request for Science was $6.304 billion, a decrease of 8.7% from FY2019. Within this total, funding for Earth Science was to decrease by $151 million (7.8%); funding for Planetary Science was to decrease by $136 million (4.9%); and funding for Astrophysics was to decrease by $347 million (29.1%). The request for Earth Science included no funding for the Pre-Aerosol, Clouds, and Ocean Ecosystem (PACE) mission or the Climate Absolute Radiance and Refractivity Observatory (CLARREO) Pathfinder mission. PACE and CLARREO Pathfinder were also proposed for termination in the FY2018 and FY2019 budgets but were funded by Congress. The request for Planetary Science included $593 million for a mission to Jupiter's moon Europa, but in contrast to prior congressional direction, the mission would launch on a commercial rocket and would not include a lander. The Planetary Science request also included $210 million for the Lunar Discovery and Exploration program, initiated in FY2019, to fund public-private partnerships for research using commercial lunar landers. The request for Astrophysics did not include funding for the Wide Field Infrared Space Telescope (WFIRST, $312 million in FY2019). The proposed increase of $48 million for the James Webb Space

---

[61] This section was written by Daniel Morgan, Specialist in Science and Technology Policy, CRS Resources, Science, and Industry Division.

[62] The additional funds requested for NASA in the budget amendment were to support an accelerated program to return U.S. astronauts to the Moon. The amendment requested funds in three NASA accounts, but did not state how the additional amounts would be allocated to budget lines within those accounts. In addition, the House committee report (H.Rept. 116-101) described its recommendations relative to the original request, without reference to the budget amendment. This section therefore discusses the original request and the budget amendment separately, rather than attempting to consolidate them into a revised Administration request.

Telescope (JWST) would have provided $155 million more for JWST in FY2020 than was projected in the FY2019 budget; this change reflected previously announced cost increases and schedule delays. The budget amendment requested an additional $90 million for Science, to support robotic exploration of the Moon's polar regions in advance of a human lunar mission.

The House bill would have provided $7.161 billion for Science, which would have been $858 million (or 14%) more than the initial request. The total included funding for PACE ($147 million), CLARREO Pathfinder ($26 million), and WFIRST ($511 million). It included the requested amount for a Europa mission without a lander component, but it directed NASA to request funding for continued R&D on a Europa lander in the FY2021 budget. It included, without comment, the requested amount for JWST. It did not include the additional funding proposed in the budget amendment.

The Senate bill would have provided $6.906 billion for Science, which would have been $602 million (or 10%) more than the initial request. The total included funding for PACE ($161 million), CLARREO Pathfinder ($18 million), and WFIRST ($446 million), as well as $70 million more than the requested amount for JWST. The Senate report did not mention the Europa mission. It did not explicitly mention the budget amendment, although it did include the amendment's additional request for Science in its stated total for the request.

The enacted appropriation for Science was $7.139 billion—$835 million (or 13%) more than the initial request. The total included funding for PACE ($131 million), CLARREO ($26 million), and WFIRST ($511 million), as well as $70 million more than the request for JWST. It included the requested amount for the Europa mission, with both a lander and an orbiter to be launched using the Space Launch System rather than commercial rockets.

The FY2020 request for Aeronautics was $667 million, a decrease of 8.0% from FY2019. The request included $104 million for the Low Boom Flight Demonstrator program, intended to demonstrate quiet supersonic flight. The House bill would have provided $700 million. House report language emphasized this program's work on hypersonics technology and electric aircraft. The Senate bill would have provided $784 million. Senate report language mentioned hypersonics and electric aircraft, alongside a variety of other topics, such as unmanned aircraft traffic management and research on advanced composites. The enacted appropriation was $784 million.

The initial FY2020 request for Exploration Technology (currently Space Technology) was $1.014 billion, an increase of 9.4% from FY2019. The request proposed $119 million for a mostly new Lunar Surface Innovation Initiative. It proposed $45 million for a restructured In-Space Robotic Servicing program, down from $180 million for the RESTORE-L robotic servicing mission in FY2019. The budget amendment requested an additional $132 million to support technology development for lunar surface activities and other aspects of a human return to the Moon.

The House bill would have provided $1.292 billion for Space Technology. This total included $180 million for RESTORE-L. It also included $125 million for nuclear thermal propulsion technology and $8 million for space-related regional economic development, neither of which was in the Administration request. It did not include the additional funding proposed in the budget amendment. The House report did not mention the Lunar Surface Innovation Initiative. It directed NASA to preserve the Space Technology Mission Directorate "as a standalone entity within the agency" and maintain its focus on "broad technology development goals that are independent of mission-specific needs."

The Senate bill would have provided $1.076 billion for Space Technology. This total included $180 million for RESTORE-L and $100 million for nuclear thermal propulsion. The Senate report did not explicitly mention the budget amendment, although it included the amendment's additional request for Exploration Technology in its stated total for the request. It stated that the Space Technology Mission Directorate "funds basic research that can advance multi-purpose technologies to enable new approaches to NASA's current missions. These technologies can serve all NASA mission directorates and are not solely focused on enabling human spaceflight." In particular, the Senate report rejected the Administration's proposal to transfer funding for the human research program from the Exploration account to the Space Technology account.

The enacted appropriation for Space Technology was $1.100 billion. The total included $180 million for RESTORE-L, $110 million for nuclear thermal propulsion, and $8 million for space-related regional economic development. The explanatory statement did not mention the Lunar Surface Innovation Initiative and gave no explicit guidance about the mission and scope of the Space Technology Mission Directorate.

The initial FY2020 request for Deep Space Exploration Systems (currently Exploration) was $5.022 billion, a decrease of 0.6% from FY2019. This account funds development of the Orion Multipurpose Crew Vehicle and the Space Launch System (SLS) heavy-lift rocket, the capsule and launch vehicle mandated by the NASA Authorization Act of 2010 for future human exploration beyond Earth orbit. At the time of the budget release, the first test flight of SLS carrying Orion but no crew (known as Artemis 1)[63] was expected no earlier than June 2020.[64] The first flight of Orion and the SLS with a crew on board (known as Artemis 2)[65] was expected by April 2023.[66] Under the request, funding for Orion, the SLS, and related ground systems (collectively known as Exploration Systems Development) was to decrease by $651 million (15.9%). The account also funds Exploration R&D, which was to increase by $622 million (64.9%). The request for Exploration R&D included $821 million for a platform in lunar orbit (known as the Gateway) to serve as a test bed for deep space human exploration capabilities. The budget amendment requested an additional $1.375 billion for Deep Space Exploration Systems to keep the SLS and Orion programs on schedule and accelerate the development of human-rated lunar lander systems. The budget amendment proposed deferring some elements of the Gateway, relative to the plans set out in the original request.

The House bill would have provided $5.130 billion for Exploration. This total included $726 million (21%) more than the initial request for Exploration Systems Development and $618 million (39%) less than the initial request for Exploration R&D. It did not include the additional funding proposed in the budget amendment. The House committee report did not specify an amount for the Gateway platform, funded in Exploration R&D, but it associated the Administration's proposed increase in Gateway funding with proposed decreases in other programs (such as PACE, CLARREO, and WFIRST) that it rejected.

The Senate bill would have provided $6.223 billion for Exploration. This total included $1.141 billion (33%) more than the initial request for Explorations Systems Development and $60 million (4%) more than the initial request for Exploration R&D, including $500 million for the Gateway. Regarding the budget amendment, the Senate committee report stated:

> The Committee has used the amended request as a guide in formulating its recommendations but also recognizes that several aspects of the accelerated mission are in

---

[63] Formerly Exploration Mission 1, or EM-1.

[64] It is now expected no earlier than November 2020. (National Aeronautics and Space Administration, Office of Inspector General, *NASA's Management of Space Launch System Program Costs and Contracts*, IG-20-012, March 10, 2020, https://oig.nasa.gov/docs/IG-20-012.pdf)

[65] Formerly EM-2.

[66] It is now scheduled for October 2022. (NASA, Office of Inspector General, *NASA's Management of Space Launch System Program Costs and Contracts*)

the early stages of planning and development, and the estimated costs of elements through completion of the near term goal were not available to the Committee. While there is support for the mission, it is difficult to weigh the impacts of the accelerated mission on the overall budget of NASA with only a single year budget proposal. NASA must provide 5-year budget profiles, similar to all other NASA missions and programs, in order to allow a thorough evaluation by the Committee. In the interim, the Committee has provided funds to allow for NASA to advance its human exploration program and awaits further definition of the program and its estimated associated costs.

The enacted appropriation for Exploration was $6.018 billion. This total included $1.141 billion (33%) more than the initial request for Explorations Systems Development and $145 million (9%) less than the initial request for Exploration R&D, including $450 million for the Gateway.

In the LEO and Spaceflight Operations account (currently Space Operations), the request for Commercial Crew was $102 million, a decrease of 41.1% from FY2019; the request for the ISS was $1.458 billion;[67] and the request for Commercial LEO Development, a new program in FY2019, was $150 million (an increase of 275.0%). The proposed reduction in Commercial Crew funding reflected the expected transition of commercial crew activities from development to operations: the first post-certification crewed flight to the ISS was planned for late FY2019.[68] The Commercial LEO Development program is intended to stimulate a commercial space economy in low Earth orbit, including the commercial provision of NASA's requirements for research and technology demonstration after the proposed end of direct ISS funding in 2025. The House bill would have provided the requested amount for the Space Operations account as a whole and for Commercial Crew within that total. The House committee report did not specify how the remainder should be allocated to the ISS, Commercial LEO Development, or other programs. The Senate bill would have provided the requested amount for Commercial Crew and $15 million for Commercial LEO Development ($135 million less than the request). The Senate committee report did not specify an allocation for the ISS, but relative to the request, its total for Space Operations as a whole was reduced by almost the same amount as its allocation for Commercial LEO Development, suggesting that the amount available for the ISS might be close to the requested level. The enacted appropriation for Space Operations included the requested amount for Commercial Crew and $15 million for Commercial LEO Development. It did not specify an amount for the ISS; as with the Senate bill, the enacted amount for the account as a whole suggests that the ISS allocation might be close to the requested level.

Table 11. National Aeronautics and Space Administration R&D

(budget authority, in millions of dollars)

	FY2019 Enacted	FY2020 Initial Request	FY2020 Budget Amdmt.[a]	FY2020 House	FY2020 Senate	FY2020 Enacted
Science	**6,906**	**6,304**	**+90**	**7,161**	**6,906**	**7,139[f]**
Earth Science	1,931	1,780		2,023	1,945	1,972
Planetary Science	2,759	2,622		2,713	2,631	2,713
Astrophysics	1,192	845		1,368	1,172	1,306
James Webb Space Telescope	305	353		353	423	423
Heliophysics	720	705		705	735	725

---

[67] The FY2019 appropriations act and conference report did not specify an FY2019 amount for the ISS.

[68] It is now expected in 2020.

	FY2019 Enacted	FY2020 Initial Request	FY2020 Budget Amdmt.[a]	FY2020 House	FY2020 Senate	FY2020 Enacted
Aeronautics	725	667		700	784	784
Space Tech. / Exploration Tech.	927	1,014	+132	1,292	1,076	1,100
Exploration / Deep Sp. Exp. Sys.	5,051	5,022	+1,375	5,130	6,223	6.018
Exploration Systems Development	4,093	3,442		4,168	4,583	4,583
Exploration R&D	958	1,580		962	1,640	1,435
Space Ops. / LEO and Spaceflight Ops.[c]	~1,678[c]	1,710[c]		~1,710[c]	~1,575[c]	~1,575[c]
International Space Station	n/s	1,458		n/s	n/s	n/s
Commercial Crew	173	102		102	102	102
Commercial LEO Development	40	150		n/s	15	15
Subtotal R&D	15,287	14,717		15,993	16,564	16,616
Non-R&D Programs[d]	3,110	2,617		2,741	2,727	2,727
Safety, Security, and Mission Services	2,755	3,085		3,085	2,935	2,913
Associated with R&D[e]	*2,289*	*2,619*		*2,633*	*2,520*	*2,503*
Construction & Environmental C&R	348	600		497	524	373
Associated with R&D[e]	*289*	*510*		*424*	*450*	*321*
NASA, Total (R&D)	17,865	17,845		19,051	19,534	19,439[f]
NASA, Total	21,500	21,019	+1,597	22,316	22,750	22,629[f]

Sources: FY2019 enacted from P.L. 116-6 and H.Rept. 116-9. Initial FY2020 request from NASA FY2020 congressional budget justification, http://www.nasa.gov/news/budget/. FY2020 budget amendment from Estimate #1, May 13, 2019, https://www.whitehouse.gov/wp-content/uploads/2019/05/FY20_Budget_Amendment_5-13-19.pdf. FY2020 House from H.R. 3055 as passed by the House and H.Rept. 116-101. Senate from H.R. 3055 as passed by the Senate and S.Rept. 116-127. Enacted from P.L. 116-93 and explanatory statement, *Congressional Record*, December 17, 2019, Book II.

Notes: Totals may differ from the sum of the components due to rounding. LEO = Low Earth Orbit. C&R = Compliance and Remediation. n/s = not specified. Figures for the column headed "FY2020 Enacted" will be added when available.

a. Budget amendment amounts are in addition to the initial request. The amendment does not state how the additional amounts would be allocated to budget lines within each account.

b. Does not reflect rescission of $70 million in unobligated prior-year balances.

c. Excluding non-R&D activities: Space and Flight Support and Space Transportation other than Commercial Crew. FY2019 amount includes CRS estimate of $1.465 billion for International Space Station for the purpose of calculating a total. For the same purpose, FY2020 House and Senate amounts are estimated based on the Administration's request for amounts shown as "n/s."

d. Non-R&D activities in Space Operations / LEO and Spaceflight Operations (see note b); STEM Engagement (formerly Education); and Inspector General.

e. CRS estimates the allocation between R&D and non-R&D in proportion to the underlying program amounts in order to allow calculation of a total for R&D. The Safety, Security, and Mission Services account and the Construction and Environmental Compliance and Remediation account consist mostly of indirect costs for other programs, assessed in proportion to their direct costs.

National Science Foundation[69]

The National Science Foundation supports basic research and education in the nonmedical sciences and engineering. Congress established the foundation as an independent federal agency in 1950 and directed it to "promote the progress of science; to advance the national health, prosperity, and welfare; to secure the national defense; and for other purposes."[70] The NSF is a primary source of federal support for U.S. university research, especially in mathematics and computer science. It is also responsible for significant shares of the federal science, technology, engineering, and mathematics (STEM) education program portfolio and federal STEM student aid and support.

NSF has six appropriations accounts: Research and Related Activities (RRA, the main research account), Education and Human Resources (EHR, the main education account), Major Research Equipment and Facilities Construction (MREFC), Agency Operations and Award Management (AOAM), the National Science Board (NSB), and the Office of Inspector General (OIG). Appropriations are generally provided at the account level, while program-specific direction may be included in appropriations acts, or accompanying conference reports or explanatory statements.

Because final FY2019 funding was not available at the time the FY2020 budget request was prepared, requested R&D funding is compared to the FY2018 actual funding. FY2019 funding levels, enacted February 15, 2019, are included for reference.[71] These amounts are available only at the account level; FY2019 R&D breakouts and subaccount funding amounts are not yet available for comparison.

Funding for R&D is included in the RRA, EHR, and MREFC accounts. (The RRA and EHR accounts also include non-R&D funding.) Together, these three accounts comprise 95% of the total requested funding for NSF. Actual R&D obligations for each account are known after NSF allocates funding appropriations to specific activities and reports those figures.[72] The budget request specifies R&D funding for the conduct of research, including basic and applied research, and for physical assets, including R&D facilities and major equipment. Funding amounts for FY2018 actual and FY2020 requested levels are reported by account, including amounts for R&D conduct and physical assets where applicable, in **Table 12**.

Overall. The Administration requested $7.07 billion for the NSF in FY2020, $1.01 billion (12.5%) less than the FY2019 enacted amount, and $752 million (9.6%) less than the FY2018 actual amount. The request would have decreased budget authority in three accounts relative to the FY2018 enacted level: RRA by $717.4 million (11.2%), EHR by $80.4 million (8.9%), and NSB by $200,000 (4.7%). The request would have increased budget authority for the MREFC account by $36.9 million (19.8%) and provided slight increases to the AOAM (2.6%, $8.4 million) and OIG (1.7%, $260,000) accounts. Overall, NSF estimated that, under the FY2020 request, agency-wide funding rates (i.e., the percentage of submitted proposals that are

---

[69] This section was written by Laurie Harris, Analyst in Science and Technology Policy, CRS Resources, Science, and Industry Division.

[70] The National Science Foundation Act of 1950 (P.L. 81-507).

[71] The Consolidated Appropriations Act, 2019 (P.L. 116-6); and Explanatory Statement, Consolidated Appropriations Act, 2019, Division C (Commerce, Justice, Science, and Related Agencies Appropriations Act, 2019), *Congressional Record*, vol. 165, no. 28—Book II (February 13, 2019), p. H1813.

[72] R&D actual (FY2018) and requested (FY2020) amounts are reported in the "Quantitative Data Tables" section of the FY2020 *NSF Budget Request to Congress*, March 18, 2019, pp. QDT-1–QDT-7.

---

successfully awarded funding) would have decreased slightly from 24% to 23%, with 1,317 fewer new competitive awards, compared to FY2018.

As a proportion of NSF's total funding, R&D activities account for approximately 81%. For FY2020, $5.72 billion was requested for R&D activities, a 10% decrease from FY2018 actual funding for R&D of $6.36 billion. The total request included $5.22 billion (91%) for the conduct of R&D, and $506 million (9%) for R&D facilities and major equipment. Of funding requested for the conduct of R&D, 87% was requested for basic research, and 13% for applied research. Overall funding for R&D facilities and major equipment supports not only the construction and acquisition phases, funded through MREFC ($223 million requested), but also the planning, design, and postconstruction operations and maintenance, funded through RRA ($282 million requested).

As passed by the House on June 25, 2019, the Commerce, Justice, Science, Agriculture, Rural Development, Food and Drug Administration, Interior, Environment, Military Construction, Veterans Affairs, Transportation, and Housing and Urban Development Appropriations Act, 2020 (H.R. 3055) would have provided a total of $8.363 billion to NSF in FY2020, a $1.570 billion (22%) increase from the requested amount, and a $561 million (7%) increase from the FY2019 enacted amount. These amounts include both R&D and non-R&D funding. As passed by the Senate on October 31, 2019, H.R. 3055 would have provided a total of $8.317 billion to NSF in FY2020, a $1.251 billion (18%) increase from the requested amount, and a $242 million (3.4%) increase from the FY2019 enacted amount. As signed by the President on December 20, 2019, the Consolidated Appropriations Act, 2020 (P.L. 116-93) provides a total of $8.278 billion to NSF for FY2020, $1.212 billion (17.7%) more than the requested amount, and $203.3 (2.5%) more than the FY2019 enacted amount.

Research. The Administration sought $5.66 billion for RRA in FY2020, an $857 million (13.1%) decrease compared to the FY2019 enacted funding, and a $717 million (11.2%) decrease compared to FY2018 actual funding. Compared to the FY2018 actual levels, the FY2020 request included decreases for 8 of the 10 RRA subaccounts. The largest percentage decrease would have gone to the Office of Polar Programs (19.6%, $98.3 million decrease). The largest percentage increase would have gone to the U.S. Arctic Research Commission account (6.3%, $90,000 increase). The FY2020 request also included $151 million for the RRA Established Program to Stimulate Competitive Research (EPSCoR) program, a $19.4 million (11.3%) decrease compared to FY2018 actual funding.

Within the RRA account, the FY2020 request included $5.08 billion for R&D, a decrease of $634 million (11.1%) compared to the FY2018 actual amount. Of this amount, the majority ($4.80 billion, 94%) was requested for the conduct of research, including $4.38 billion for basic research and $417 million for applied research.

As passed by the House, H.R. 3055 would have provided a total of $7.106 billion for RRA, $1.443 billion (25%) more than the request, and $586 million (9%) more than the FY2019 enacted amount. As passed by the Senate, H.R. 3055 would have provided a total of $6.770 billion for RRA, $1.107 billion (20%) more than the request, and $250 million (4%) more than the FY2019 enacted amount. P.L. 116-93 provides $6.770 billion for RRA, $1.074 billion (19.0%) more than the request, and $2.17 billion (3.3%) more than the FY2019 enacted amount.

Education. The FY2020 request for the EHR account was $86.5 million (9.5%) less than the FY2019 enacted amount and $80.4 million (8.9%) less than the FY2018 actual level. By program division, the Division of Human Resource Development would have received an increase of $15.6 million (9.6%) over the FY2018 actual level. The divisions of research on learning in formal and informal settings, graduate education, and undergraduate education would have received decreases of 20.4% ($182 million requested), 5.5% ($244 million requested), and 13.8% ($219 million requested), respectively.

EHR programs of particular interest to congressional policymakers include the Graduate Research Fellowship Program (GRFP) and National Research Traineeship (NRT) programs. The FY2020 request for GRFP was $257 million, a reduction of $27.9 million (9.8%) from the FY2018 actual level. The FY2020 request for NRT was $49.5 million, a $4.3 million (8.0%) decrease from FY2018.

Within EHR, requested funding for R&D was $420 million, which is $37.7 million (8.2%) less than the FY2018 actual funding amount and accounts for approximately 7.3% of the agency's total R&D request. All of the requested funding would support the conduct of R&D, including $150 million for basic research and $270 million for applied research.

As passed by the House, H.R. 3055 would have provided a total of $950 million for EHR, $127 million (15%) more than the request, and $40 million (4%) more than the FY2019 enacted amount. As passed by the Senate, H.R. 3055 would have provided a total of $937 million for EHR, $114 million (14%) more than the request, and $27 million (3%) more than the FY2019 enacted amount. P.L. 116-93 provides $940 million for EHR, $116 million (14.2%) more than the FY2020 request, and $30 million (3.3%) more than the FY2019 enacted amount.

Construction. The MREFC account supports large construction projects and scientific instruments, with all of the funding supporting R&D facilities. The Administration sought $223 million for MREFC in FY2020, $36.9 million (19.8%) more than the FY2018 enacted amount, and $72.5 million (24.5%) less than the FY2018 actual amount.

Requested MREFC funding would support continued construction of the Large Synoptic Survey Telescope (LSST, $46.3 million requested, 5.1% decrease from FY2019 enacted) and Antarctic Infrastructure Modernization for Science (AIMS, $97.9 million requested, 5.6% decrease from FY2019 enacted). The request included $33.0 million for upgrades to the Large Hadron Collider in Switzerland, which would represent the first year of a five-year project. Additionally, $45.0 million was requested for Mid-scale Research Infrastructure projects in the $20 million to $70 million range; this is a new funding line-item in the MREFC account meant to manage support for upgrades to major facilities and stand-alone projects in this range as a portfolio.

As passed by the House, H.R. 3055 would have provided a total of $223 million for MREFC, equal to the request, and $73 million (25%) less than the FY2019 enacted amount. As passed by the Senate, H.R. 3055 would have provided a total of $253 million for MREFC, $30 million (13%) more than the request, and $43 million (14%) less than the FY2019 enacted amount. P.L. 116-93 provides $243 million for MREFC, $20 million (9%) more than the request, and $52 million (18%) less than the FY2019 enacted amount.

Other initiatives. The FY2020 NSF budget request included funding for three multiagency initiatives. This funding is included in multiple NSF appropriations accounts, and R&D amounts are not separately provided. The National Nanotechnology Initiative would have received $389 million, $179 million (31.4%) less than in FY2018. The Networking and Information Technology Research and Development program would have received $1.20 billion, a decrease of $98.2 million (7.6%). The U.S. Global Change Research Program would have received $224 million, $30.0 million (11.8%) less than in FY2018.[73]

---

[73] For additional information on these initiatives, see "Multiagency R&D Initiatives."

Table 12. National Science Foundation Funding

(budget authority, in millions of dollars)

Account	FY2018 Actual	FY2019 Enacted	FY2020 Request	FY2020 House	FY2020 Senate	FY2020 Enacted
Research and Related Activities (RRA)	**6,380.4**	**6,520.0**	**5,663.0**	**7,106.3**	**6,769.7**	**6,737.2**
R&D, RRA Total	5,714.1	n/a	5,079.7	n/a	n/a	n/a
Conduct of R&D	*5,391.8*	*n/a*	*4,797.3*	*n/a*	*n/a*	*n/a*
R&D Facilities and Major Equipment	*322.3*	*n/a*	*282.4*	*n/a*	*n/a*	*n/a*
Education and Human Resources (EHR)	**903.9**	**910.0**	**823.5**	**950.0**	**937.0**	**940.0**
R&D, EHR Total	457.7	n/a	420.0	n/a	n/a	n/a
Conduct of R&D	*457.7*	*n/a*	*420.0*	*n/a*	*n/a*	*n/a*
R&D Facilities and Major Equipment	*0.0*	*n/a*	*0.0*	*n/a*	*n/a*	*n/a*
Major Research Equipment and Facilities Construction (MREFC)	**186.3**	**295.7**	**223.2**	**223.2**	**253.2**	**243.2**
R&D, MREFC Total	186.3	n/a	223.2	n/a	n/a	n/a
Conduct of R&D	*0.0*	*n/a*	*0.0*	*n/a*	*n/a*	*n/a*
R&D Facilities and Major Equipment	*186.3*	*n/a*	*223.2*	*n/a*	*n/a*	*n/a*
Agency Operations and Award Management (AOAM)[a]	**328.5**	**329.5**	**336.9**	**336.9**	**336.9**	**336.9**
National Science Board (NSB)[a]	**4.3**	**4.4**	**4.1**	**4.4**	**4.5**	**4.5**
Office of the Inspector General (OIG)[a]	**15.1**	**15.4**	**15.4**	**15.4**	**15.7**	**16.5**
NSF, Total Discretionary[b]	**7,818.4**	**8,075.0**	**7,066.0**	**8,636.1**	**8,317.0**	**8,278.3**
R&D, NSF Total	6,358.0	n/a	5,722.9	n/a	n/a	n/a
Total, Conduct of R&D	*5,849.5*	*n/a*	*5,217.3*	*n/a*	*n/a*	*n/a*
Total, R&D Facilities & Major Equipment	*508.6*	*n/a*	*505.6*	*n/a*	*n/a*	*n/a*

Sources: Data in the columns titled, "FY2018 Actual" and "FY2020 Request" are from the FY2020 *NSF Budget Request to Congress*. Data in the "FY2019 Enacted" column are from P.L. 116-6. Data from the FY2020 Enacted column are from P.L. 116-93.

Notes: Appropriations accounts are in bold. NSF total may differ from the sum of the accounts due to rounding. Nonbold R&D funding amounts are a subset of funding for the specified accounts. Funding amounts in the "FY2020 House" and "FY2020 Senate" columns are from Division A, Title III, of the Commerce, Justice, Science, Agriculture, Rural Development, Food and Drug Administration, Interior, Environment, Military Construction, Veterans Affairs, Transportation, and Housing and Urban Development Appropriations Act, 2020 (H.R. 3055), as passed by the House on June 25, 2019, and the Senate on October 31, 2019. n/a = not available.

a. The AOAM, NSB, and OIG accounts have no reported R&D funding.

b. In addition to discretionary funding, NSF reports mandatory funding from H-1B visa and donation sources, which are not included in this total.

Department of Agriculture[74]

The U.S. Department of Agriculture (USDA) was created in 1862, to support agricultural research in an expanding, agriculturally dependent country. Today, USDA conducts intramural research at

---

[74] This section was written by Tadlock Cowan, Analyst in Natural Resources and Rural Development, CRS Resources, Science, and Industry Division.

federal facilities with federally employed scientists and supports extramural research at universities and other facilities through competitive grants and formula-based funding. The breadth of contemporary USDA research spans traditional agricultural production techniques, organic and sustainable agriculture, bioenergy, nutrition needs and food composition, food safety, animal and plant health, pest and disease management, economic decisionmaking, and other social sciences affecting consumers, farmers, and rural communities.

Four agencies carry out USDA's intramural and extramural research and education activities, grouped together into the Research, Education, and Economics (REE) mission area. The agencies involved are the Agricultural Research Service (ARS), the principal intramural research agency, National Institute of Food and Agriculture (NIFA), the principal extramural research agency, National Agricultural Statistics Service (NASS), and Economic Research Service (ERS).

For FY2020, Division B of the Further Consolidated Appropriations Act (P.L. 116-94) provides a total of $3,399.7 million for USDA's Research, Education, and Economics mission area. This is $24.4 million less than enacted for FY2019 (-0.7%). The Senate-passed FY2020 appropriations bill (H.R. 3055) recommended a total of $3,476.5 million in discretionary spending for the four agencies in FY2020, and the House-passed bill recommended $3,283.2 million (see **Table 13**). In addition to discretionary federal appropriations, agricultural research is funded by state matching contributions and private donations or grants, as well as certain mandatory funding authorized by the farm bill.[75] The FY2020 enacted discretionary appropriations are discussed below.

Agricultural Research Service

The Agricultural Research Service is USDA's in-house basic and applied research agency, and has major responsibilities for conducting and leading the national agricultural research effort. It operates approximately 90 laboratories nationwide with about 6,600 employees. ARS laboratories focus on efficient food and fiber production, development of new products and uses for agricultural commodities, development of effective controls for pest management, and support of USDA regulatory and technical assistance programs. ARS also operates the Abraham Lincoln National Agricultural Library, one of the department's primary information repositories for food, agriculture, and natural resource sciences.

For FY2020, P.L. 116-94 will provide $1,414.4 million for ARS salaries and expenses ($111.1 million more than FY2019) and $192.7 million for buildings and facilities ($188.5 million less than FY2019). The Administration had requested $1,203.5 million for ARS salaries and expenses for FY2020, and $50.0 million for the buildings and facilities account (**Table 13**). The enacted bill does not support the Administration's request regarding termination of various research programs and the closure of certain ARS laboratories. The enacted bill also directs ARS to fill various vacant positions in ARS laboratories, and encourages them to do so with permanent employees.

ARS assumes ownership of the National Bio and Agro-Defense Facility (NBAF) in FY2019 from the Department of Homeland Security (DHS). The FY2019 enacted bill provided $10.6 million to address one-time costs associated with the transfer of the science program from the Plum Island Animal Disease Center to NBAF, and $42.0 million to address stand-up activities and other initial costs to operate and maintain the new facility. NBAF is expected to be fully operational by December 31, 2022. P.L. 116-94 provides $13.1million for NBAF transition and equipment purchases in FY2020.

---

[75] For additional information, see CRS Report R45974, *Agriculture and Related Agencies: FY2020 Appropriations*, by Jim Monke.

National Institute of Food and Agriculture

The National Institute of Food and Agriculture (NIFA) is USDA's principal extramural research agency. NIFA provides federal funding for research, education, and extension projects conducted in partnership with State Agricultural Experiment Stations, the State Cooperative Extension System, land grant universities, colleges, and other research and education institutions, as well as individual researchers. These partnerships include the 1862 land-grant institutions, 1890 historically black colleges and universities (HBCUs) established by the Morrill Acts, the 1994 tribal land-grant colleges, and Hispanic-serving institutions.[76] Federal funds enhance research capacity at universities and institutions through statutory formula funding, competitive awards, and grants.[77]

The FY 2020 enacted bill provides a total of $1,527.5 million for NIFA research, education, and extension activities. This is $56.2 million more (3.8%) than was enacted in FY2019, and $135.8 million more (9.7%) than requested by the Administration (**Table 13**). The enacted bill provides $259.0 million for Hatch Act formula funding for 1862 land grant university research and education activities, the same as enacted for FY2019. For Evans-Allen formula funding to the 19 HBCUs, P.L. 116-94 provides $67.0 million for research, $9.0 million more than in FY2019 (15.5%).

For research grants to the 1994 Tribal institutions, the enacted bill provides $3.8 million, the same as the enacted amount for FY2019. The bill also provides $11.9 million for the Native American Institutions Endowment Fund, the same as the House bill, the Administration's request, and the amount enacted for FY2019. For education grants to Hispanic-serving institutions, P.L. 116-94 provides $11.2 million.

For McIntire-Stennis cooperative forestry research support, P.L. 116-94 will provide $36.0 million for FY2020, the same as for FY2019. The Administration had requested $28.9 million for FY2020. The enacted bill provides $425.0 million for the Agriculture and Food Research Initiative (AFRI)—USDA's flagship competitive research grants program. This is $10.0 million more than FY2019. The Administration had requested $500.0 million for the program in FY2020, a 20.5% increase over FY2019. This budget item currently represents about 28% of the total NIFA discretionary budget.

For Cooperative Extension support at 1862 land grant universities under the Smith-Lever Act, the Senate-passed bill recommends $315.0 million for Sections (b) and (c) formula funding for FY2020, the same as enacted for FY2019. The Administration had requested $299.4 million for these programs in FY2020. The Smith-Lever Sections (b) and (c) programs include extension services at the HBCUs and the 1994 Tribal colleges, and women and minorities in STEM fields, among other programs. The bill provides $57.9 million and $8.0 million respectively for extension activities at HBCUs and 1994 tribal colleges.

P.L. 116-94 will provide $87.8 million for Smith-Lever 3(d) activities, including food and nutrition education, new technologies for agricultural extension, and children, youth, and families at risk, and includes $70.0 million for the Expanded Food and Nutrition Education Program. The bill also provides $3.2 million to support Federally-Recognized Tribes Extension programs on

---

[76] The numbers 1862, 1890, and 1994 in this context refer to the years that laws were enacted creating these classifications of colleges and universities, not to the number of institutions. For more detailed information on the land-grant colleges and universities see CRS Report R45897, *The U.S. Land-Grant University System: An Overview*, by Genevieve K. Croft.

[77] The National Agricultural Research, Extension, and Teaching Policy Act of 1977 designated USDA as the lead federal agency for higher education in the food and agricultural sciences.

American Indian Reservations and Tribal jurisdictions and $8.4 million for Children, Youth, and Families at Risk. The Administration had requested $0 funding in FY2020 for other Smith-Lever Section 3(d) programs.

National Agricultural Statistics Service

The National Agricultural Statistics Service conducts the quinquennial Census of Agriculture and provides official statistics on agricultural production and indicators of the economic and environmental status of the farm sector.

The enacted bill provides a total of $180.3 million for NASS in FY2020, $45.3 of which is reserved for the 2017 Census of Agriculture and Current Industrial Report surveys. The support for the Census is the same as enacted for FY2019. The Administration had requested $163.0 million for NASS in FY2020, and up to $45.3 million to support NASS's Census activity. Initial results of the 2017 Census of Agriculture were released on April 11, 2019. The enacted bill does not accept any proposed eliminations of ongoing activities, such as certain crop surveys, and recommends $2.0 million to expand the Farm Labor Survey, $1,000,000 for the Agriculture and Rural Prosperity Initiative, and $2,000,000 to strengthen NASS activities in support of the National Animal Health Monitoring System, commodity studies, and the Agricultural Resource Management Survey.

Economic Research Service

The Economic Research Service supports economic and social science analysis about agriculture, rural development, food, commodity markets, and the environment. It also collects and disseminates data concerning USDA programs and policies. ERS is one of 13 "principal statistical agencies" of the Federal Statistical System of the United States.[78]

For FY2020, P.L. 116-94 provides $84.8 million for ERS, $2.0 million less (-2.3%) than enacted for FY2019. The Administration had requested $60.5 million for ERS in FY2020, a 30.3% decrease from FY2019.

---

[78] In June 2019, the Secretary announced plans to relocate ERS and NIFA from Washington, DC, to the Kansas City region. The FY2020 House-passed appropriation bill prohibits any funding for costs associated with the proposed move of the agencies. The Senate bill did not contain language prohibiting any funding for the move. The move is projected to be completed by December 2019. For further information on the proposed relocation of ERS and NIFA, see CRS In Focus IF11166, *Proposed Relocation/Realignment of USDA's ERS and NIFA*, by Tadlock Cowan.

Table 13. U.S. Department of Agriculture R&D

(budget authority, in millions of dollars)

Agency or Major Program	FY2019 Enacted P.L. 116-6	FY2020 Request	FY2020 House	FY2020 Senate	FY2020 Enacted
Agricultural Research Service					
Salaries and Expenses	1,303.3	1,203.5	1,347.5	1,424.9	1,414.4
Buildings and Facilities	381.2	50.0	50.0	304.8	192.7
Other	7.0	0.0	0.0	0.0	0.0
Subtotal, ARS	**1,691.5**	**1,253.5**	**1,397.5**	**1,729.7**	**1607.1**
National Institute of Food and Agriculture (NIFA)					
Research and Education					
AFRI (competitive grants)	415.0	500.0	460.0	425.0	425.0
Hatch Act (1862 institutions)	259.0	243.2	265.0	259.0	259.0
Evans-Allen (1890 institutions)	58.0	53.8	67.0	58.0	67.0
McIntire-Stennis (forestry)	36.0	28.9	38.0	36.0	36.0
Other	159.6	148.8	205.0	159.6	175.9
Subtotal	**927.6**	**974.7**	**1,035.0**	**937.6**	**962.9**
Extension					
Smith-Lever (b) and (c)	315.0	299.4	325.0	315.0	315.0
Smith-Lever (d)	86.6	58.1	86.8	88.0	87.8
1890 Extension Activities	48.6	47.3	57.0	48.6	57.0
1994 Extension Activities	6.4	4.4	8.0	6.4	8.0
Other	49.1	6.1	65.3	51.1	58.8
Subtotal	**505.7**	**415.3**	**542.1**	**509.1**	**526.6**
Integrated Activities	***38.0***	***1.7***	***40.0***	***38.0***	***38.0***
Subtotal, NIFA	**1,471.3**	**1,391.7**	**1,617.1**	**1,484.7**	**1,527.5**
National Agricultural Statistics Service (NASS)	**174.5**	**163.0**	**180.8**	**175.3**	**180.3**
Economic Research Service (ERS)	**86.8**	**60.5**	**87.8**	**86.8**	**84.8**
Total, USDA Research, Education, and Economics Mission Area	**3,424.1**	**2,868.7**	**3,283.2**	**3,476.5**	**3,399.7**

Sources: CRS, compiled from P.L. 116-6; Conf. Rept. 116-9; H.R. 3055; H. Rept. 116-107, H. Rept. 116-110; P.L 116-94, Division B (The House Rules Committee released an Explanatory Statement for the Further Consolidated Appropriations Act, including Division B, at https://rules.house.gov/bill/116/hr-1865-sa); *Omnibus Appropriation Explanatory Statement, Division A; 2020 USDA Budget Justification Notes.* .

Department of Commerce

Two agencies of the Department of Commerce have major R&D programs: the National Institute of Standards and Technology (NIST) and the National Oceanic and Atmospheric Administration (NOAA).

National Institute of Standards and Technology[79]

The mission of the National Institute of Standards and Technology is "to promote U.S. innovation and industrial competitiveness by advancing measurement science, standards, and technology in ways that enhance economic security and improve our quality of life."[80] NIST research provides measurement, calibration, and quality assurance methods and techniques that support U.S. commerce, technological progress, product reliability, manufacturing processes, and public safety. NIST's responsibilities include the development, maintenance, and custodial retention of the national standards of measurement; providing the means and methods for making measurements consistent with those standards; and ensuring the compatibility of U.S. national measurement standards with those of other nations.[81]

The President requested $686.8 million for NIST in FY2020, a decrease of $298.7 million (30.3%) from the FY2019 enacted appropriation of $985.5 million. (See **Table 14**.) NIST discretionary funding is provided through three accounts: Scientific and Technical Research and Services (STRS), Industrial Technology Services (ITS), and Construction of Research Facilities (CRF).

The President's FY2020 request included $611.7 million for R&D, standards coordination, and related services in the STRS account, a decrease of $112.8 million (15.6%) from the FY2019 level.[82]

The FY2020 request would have provided $15.2 million for the ITS account, down $139.8 million (90.2%) from FY2019. Within the ITS account, the request would have provided no funding for the Manufacturing Extension Partnership (MEP) program, a reduction of $140.0 million from FY2019; MEP centers in each state would be required to become entirely self-supporting. In his FY2019 request, President Trump proposed ending federal funding for MEP; in his FY2018 request, the President sought $6.0 million "for an orderly shutdown of the program." The request provides $15.2 million provided for Manufacturing USA (also referred to as the National Network for Manufacturing Innovation or NNMI), slightly higher than the FY2019 level of $15.0 million. Of these funds, approximately $10 million would be for continued support of the NIST-sponsored National Institute for Innovation in Manufacturing Biopharmaceuticals (NIIMBL), with the balance (approximately $5 million) to be used for coordination of the Manufacturing USA network.[83]

---

[79] This section was written by John F. Sargent Jr., Specialist in Science and Technology Policy, CRS Resources, Science, and Industry Division.

[80] NIST website, "General Information," http://nist.gov/public_affairs/general_information.cfm.

[81] 15 U.S.C. §272.

[82] CRS analysis of data from U.S. Department of Commerce, National Institute of Standards and Technology, National Institute of Standards and Technology/National Technical Information Service, Fiscal Year 2020 Budget Submission to Congress, p. NIST-5, https://www.commerce.gov/sites/default/files/2019-03/fy2020_nist_congressional_budget_justification.pdf.

[83] Ibid.

In his FY2020 budget, the President requested $59.9 million for the NIST CRF account, down $46.1 million (43.5%) from the FY2019 enacted level.[84] In addition, elsewhere in the budget, the President requested mandatory funding for a GSA Federal Capital Revolving Fund that would have provided, among other things, an additional $288.0 million in funding for NIST construction activity in FY2020 to be paid back to the fund over 15 years from future discretionary appropriations.[85] However, the Congressional Budget Office (CBO) estimated this proposal in a manner consistent with current practice that capital expenditures are recorded on a cash basis in the federal budget, scoring the $288.0 million as a request for NIST discretionary spending for FY2020. In including this, CBO excluded $19.2 million from the original ITS request which was intended to as an installment payment on the revolving fund. Therefore, the total CRF request, as calculated by CBO, was $328.7 million.

On June 19, 2019, the House passed the Commerce, Justice, Science, Agriculture, Rural Development, Food and Drug Administration, Interior, Environment, Military Construction, Veterans Affairs, Transportation, and Housing and Urban Development Appropriations Act, 2020 (H.R. 3055). Division A of the bill would provide $1.040 billion for NIST, including:

- $751.0 million for the STRS account, $26.5 million (3.7%) above the FY2019 enacted level and $139.3 million (22.8%) above the request;

- $169.2 million for the ITS account, $14.2 million (9.1%) above the FY2019 enacted level and $154.0 million (1,013%) above the request;

  - of the ITS funds $154.0 million is for the MEP program (up $14.0 million (10.0%) from the FY2019 enacted level and $154.0 million from the request), and $15.2 million is for the Manufacturing USA program (up $0.2 million (1.1%) from the FY2019 enacted level an equal to the request); and

- $120.0 million for the CRF account, up $14.0 million (13.2%) from the FY2019 enacted level and up $60.1 million (100.3%) from the request.

Of particular note, the House-passed bill effectively rejects the Administration's request to defund the MEP program, and instead provides a 10.0% increase. Funding for the Manufacturing USA program includes $10.0 million to support NIST's institute, the National Institute for Innovation in Manufacturing Biopharmaceuticals as well as $5.2 million to support the network of institutes that are part of Manufacturing USA.

On October 31, 2019, the Senate passed the Commerce, Justice, Science, Agriculture, Rural Development, Food and Drug Administration, Interior, Environment, Transportation, and Housing and Urban Development Appropriations Act, 2020 (H.R. 3055). Unlike the House-passed version, this bill does not include a division for Military Construction, and Veterans Affairs. Division A of the bill would provide $1.038 billion for NIST, including:

- $753.5 million for the STRS account, $29.0 million (4.0%) above the FY2019 enacted level, $141.8 million (23.2%) above the request, and $2.5 million (0.3%) above the House-passed level;

---

[84] Ibid.

[85] According to the NIST FY2020 budget justification, "NIST's Building 1 project at the Boulder campus has been identified as a candidate project to be funded through the GSA Federal Capital Revolving Fund [that was proposed in the President's FY2020 budget]. The Fund would provide up-front funding, estimated to be $288.0 million, to renovate Wing 5, Wing 4, Spine, Wing 1, Wing 2 and a portion of the Headhouse (auditorium, library, front lobby, conference rooms, police dispatch, and cafeteria). At the FY 2020 base funding level, NIST would repay this GSA revolving fund through annual discretionary appropriations in 15 annual payments of $19.2 million."

- $161.5 million for the ITS account, $6.5 million (4.2%) above the FY2019 enacted level, $146.3 million (962.5%) above the request, and $7.7 million (4.6%) below the House-passed level;

  - of the ITS funds $145.5 million is for the MEP program (up $5.5 million (3.9%) from the FY2019 enacted level, up $145.5 million from the request, and down $8.5 million (5.5%) from the House-passed level), and $16.0 million is for the Manufacturing USA program (up $1.0 million (6.7%) from the FY2019 enacted level, up $0.8 million (5.3%) from both the request and the House-passed level).

- $123.0 million for the CRF account, up $17.0 million (16.0%) from the FY2019 enacted level, up $63.1 million (105.3%) from the request, and up $3.0 million (2.5%) from the House-passed level.

As with the House-passed bill, the Senate-passed bill effectively rejects the Administration's request to defund the MEP program, and instead provides a 3.9% increase.

In December 2019, Congress enacted the FY2020 Consolidated Appropriations Act (H.R. 1158, P.L. 116-93) providing $1,034.0 billion for NIST for FY2020, an increase of $48.5 million (4.9%) above the FY2019 level and $78.4 million (8.2%) above President Trump's request.

P.L. 116-93 provides:

- $754.0 million for the STRS account for FY2020, $29.5 million (4.1%) above the FY2019 level and $142.3 million (23.3%) above the request;

- $162.0 million for ITS for FY2020, including $146.0 million for the MEP program, rejecting the Administration's request to defund the MEP program, and providing $6.0 million (4.3%) more than for FY2019. ITS funding includes $16.0 million for Manufacturing USA for continued support of the NIST-sponsored National Institute for Innovation in Manufacturing Biopharmaceuticals and coordination of the Manufacturing USA network; and

- $118 million for CRF, an increase of $12.0 million (11.3%) above the FY2019 level and $$210.7 million (64.1%) below the CBO calculated request level.

Table 14. National Institute of Standards and Technology Funding

(budget authority, in millions of dollars)

Budget Account	FY2019 Enacted	FY2020 Request	FY2020 House	FY2020 Senate	FY2020 Enacted
Scientific and Technical Research and Services	$724.5	$611.7	$751.0	$753.5	$754.0
Industrial Technology Services	155.0	15.2	169.2	161.5	162.0
Manufacturing Extension Partnership	*140.0*	*0.0*	*154.0*	*145.5*	*146.0*
Network for Manufacturing Innovation	*15.0*	*15.2*	*15.2*	*16.0*	*16.0*
Construction of Research Facilities	106.0	40.7[a]	120.0	123.0	118.0
Construction of Research Facilities, transfer from proposed GSA Federal Capital Revolving Fund	—	288.0[b]	—	—	—
NIST, Total	**$985.5**	**$955.6**	**$1,040.2**	**$1,038.0**	**$1,034.0**

Source: The FY2019 enacted amounts are from H.Rept. 116-9. The Administration's request figures are from H.Rept. 116-101. House figures are from the House-passed version of H.R. 3055. The Senate figures are from the Senate-passed version of H.R. 3055. The enacted figures are from P.L. 116-93.

Note: Columns may not add to totals due to rounding.

a. NIST's original request of $59.9 million has been reduced by $19.2 million as a result of the Congressional Budget Office (CBO) interpretation and estimation described in note b.

b. According to the NIST FY2020 budget justification, "NIST's Building 1 project at the Boulder campus has been identified as a candidate project to be funded through the GSA Federal Capital Revolving Fund [that was proposed in the President's FY2020 budget]. The Fund would provide up-front funding, estimated to be $288.0 million, to renovate Wing 5, Wing 4, Spine, Wing 1, Wing 2 and a portion of the Headhouse (auditorium, library, front lobby, conference rooms, police dispatch, and cafeteria). At the FY 2020 base funding level, NIST would repay this GSA revolving fund through annual discretionary appropriations in 15 annual payments of $19.2 million." However, the CBO estimated this proposal in a manner consistent with current practice that capital expenditures are recorded on a cash basis in the federal budget. (For more information, see https://www.cbo.gov/system/files/115th-congress-2017-2018/reports/53461-cashaccrualmeasures.pdf.)

c. The NIST FY2020 budget justification notes, "The budgetary resources from offsetting collections for the NIST Public Safety Communications Research Fund will obligate over several fiscal years." (These funds are not included in the table figures.) These funds were provided through the NIST Public Safety Communications Research Fund to help develop wireless technologies for public safety users, as part of the National Wireless Initiative included in the Middle Class Tax Relief and Job Creation Act of 2012 (P.L. 112-96). This act provides mandatory funds for NIST from spectrum auction proceeds to help industry and public safety organizations conduct research and develop new standards, technologies, and applications to advance public safety communications in support of the initiative's efforts to build an interoperable nationwide broadband network for first responders. The act provided NIST a total of $300 million, though rescissions reduced this amount to $285 million.

National Oceanic and Atmospheric Administration[86]

The National Oceanic and Atmospheric Administration (NOAA) conducts scientific research in areas such as ecosystems, atmosphere, global climate change, weather, and oceans; collects and provides data on the oceans and atmosphere; and manages coastal and marine organisms and environments. NOAA was created in 1970 by Reorganization Plan No. 4.[87] The reorganization was intended to unify elements of the nation's environmental programs and to provide a systematic approach for monitoring, analyzing, and protecting the environment.

NOAA's administrative structure is organized into six line offices: the National Ocean Service (NOS); National Marine Fisheries Service (NMFS); National Environmental Satellite, Data, and Information Service (NESDIS); National Weather Service (NWS); Office of Oceanic and Atmospheric Research (OAR); and the Office of Marine and Aviation Operations (OMAO). The line offices are supported by an additional office, Mission Support, which provides cross-cutting administrative functions related to education, planning, information technology, human resources, and infrastructure. Congress provides most of the discretionary funding for the line offices and Mission Support through two accounts: (1) Operations, Research, and Facilities, and (2) Procurement, Acquisition, and Construction.

In 2010, NOAA published its *Next Generation Strategic Plan.*[88] The strategic plan is organized into four categories of long-term goals: (1) climate adaptation and mitigation, (2) a weather-ready

---

[86] This section was written by Eva Lipiec, Analyst in Natural Resources Policy, CRS Resources, Science, and Industry Division.

[87] "Reorganization Plan No. 4 of 1970," 35 *Federal Register* 15627-15630, October 6, 1970.

[88] National Oceanic and Atmospheric Administration (NOAA), *NOAA's Next-Generation Strategic Plan*, Silver Spring, MD, December 2010, at https://www.performance.noaa.gov/wp-content/uploads/NOAA_NGSP.pdf.

nation, (3) healthy oceans, and (4) resilient coastal communities and economies.[89] The strategic plan also lists three groups of enterprise objectives related to (1) stakeholder engagement, (2) data and observations, and (3) integrated environmental modeling.[90] The strategic plan serves as a guide for NOAA's R&D plan. The most recent R&D plan was published in 2013, and includes R&D objectives to reach strategic plan goals and objectives and targets to track progress toward R&D objectives over time.[91] NOAA released a draft 2020-2026 R&D plan in June 2019. The plan identifies three vision areas: (1) reducing societal impacts from severe weather and other environmental phenomena, (2) sustainable use and stewardship of ocean and coastal resources, and (3) a robust and effective research, development, and transition enterprise.[92] It is unclear when the draft plan will be finalized.[93]

For FY2020, President Trump requested $651.1 million in R&D funding for NOAA, a decrease of $286.9 million (30.6%) below the FY2019 enacted level of $938.0 million.[94] The President's request for total R&D was 14.6% of the total FY2020 NOAA requested amount of $4.456 billion.[95] In P.L. 116-93, Congress appropriated $972.0 million in R&D funding to NOAA for FY2020: $320.8 million (49.3%) above the FY2020 requested amount, $33.9 million (3.6%) above the FY2019 enacted level, and 18.2% of the total FY2020 NOAA enacted amount of $5.352 billion.[96] P.L. 116-93 provides $575.8 million for research (59.2% of the total enacted for NOAA R&D), $149.6 million for development (15.4%), and $246.5 million (25.4%) for R&D equipment and facilities.[97] **Table 15** provides R&D amounts enacted in FY2019, requested by the Administration for FY2020, proposed in House-passed H.R. 3055 and Senate-passed S. 2584, and enacted in FY2020 for each NOAA line office.

OAR accounts for the majority of R&D in most years, including FY2020. The President requested $335.1 million for OAR R&D in FY2020, a decrease of $196.2 million (36.9%) below

---

[89] According to NOAA, a weather-ready nation is envisioned as a society that is prepared for and responds to weather-related events.

[90] NOAA defines the enterprise objectives as "cross-cutting requirements for addressing NOAA's strategic goals as a whole." NOAA, *NOAA's Next-Generation Strategic Plan*, Silver Spring, MD, December 2010, p. 32.

[91] NOAA, *Research and Development at NOAA, Five-Year Research and Development Plan 2013-2017*, 2014, at http://nrc.noaa.gov/CouncilProducts/ResearchPlans/5YearRDPlan/NOAA5YRPHome/Preface/Purpose.aspx. NOAA's Research Council is charged with developing the five-year research and development plans. According to NOAA, "The NOAA Research Council is an internal body composed of senior scientific personnel from every line office in the agency who provide corporate oversight to ensure NOAA's research and development activities are of the highest quality, meet near- to long-term mission requirements and societal needs, take advantage of emerging scientific and technological opportunities, shape a forward-looking research agenda, and are accomplished in an efficient and cost-effective manner." NOAA, "NOAA Research Council," at http://nrc.noaa.gov.

[92] NOAA, *NOAA Research and Development Plan, 2020-2026, Draft,* June 2019, at https://nrc.noaa.gov/LinkClick.aspx?fileticket=omoYjsC59Gs%3d&portalid=0.

[93] The Federal Register Notice requesting public comment for the NOAA Research and Development Plan stated that the plan would be "set for release in 2019." The plan has not yet been publically released as of February 14, 2020. NOAA, "Research and Development Enterprise Committee (RDEC); Public Comment for the NOAA Research and Development Plan," 84 *Federal Register* 33240, July 12, 2019.

[94] Email correspondence with the NOAA Budget Office, April 8, 2019.

[95] NOAA, *Budget Estimates Fiscal Year 2020*, 2019, at https://www.corporateservices.noaa.gov/nbo/fy20_bluebook/NOAA-FY20-Congressional-Justification.pdf, p. Control Table–16. Hereafter referred to as NOAA, *Budget Estimates Fiscal Year 2020*.

[96] Email correspondence with the NOAA Budget Office, January 23, 2020 and "Explanatory Statement Submitted by Mrs. Lowey, Chairwoman of the House Committee on Appropriations Regarding H.R. 1158, Consolidated Appropriations Act, 2020," *Congressional Record*, vol. 165, no. 204, part II (December 17, 2019). Hereafter referred to as *Explanatory Statement Regarding* H.R. 1158.

[97] Email correspondence with the NOAA Budget Office, January 23, 2020.

---

the FY2019 enacted funding level of $531.4 million.[98] P.L. 116-93 provides $552.6 million for OAR R&D, an increase of $21.3 million (4.0%) from the FY2019 enacted amount and $217.5 million (64.9%) more than the FY2020 request.[99] The FY2020 enacted amount is $54.5 million (9.0%) less than proposed in H.R. 3055 and $18.7 million (3.5%) greater than proposed in S. 2584.[100]

OAR conducts research in three major areas: (1) weather and air chemistry; (2) climate; and (3) oceans, coasts, and the Great Lakes. A significant portion of these efforts is implemented through OAR's laboratories and cooperative research institutes. The President requested $169.6 million for OAR labs and cooperative institutes, $13.1 million (7.2%) less than the FY2019 enacted funding level of $182.8 million.[101] P.L. 116-93 provides $184.0 million for OAR laboratories and cooperative institutes, an increase of $1.2 million (0.7%) from the FY2019 enacted amount and $14.3 million (8.5%) more than the FY2020 request.[102] The FY2020 enacted amount is also a decrease of $7.6 million (4.0%) from the proposed amount in H.R. 3055 and an increase of $7.2 million (4.1%) from the proposed amount in S. 2584.[103]

Among other R&D activities, the President requested to terminate federal support of the National Sea Grant College Program and its related Marine Aquaculture Research program in FY2020.[104] The National Sea Grant College Program is composed of 33 university-based state programs and supports scientific research and stakeholder engagement to identify and solve problems faced by coastal communities. P.L. 116-93 provides $74.0 million to the National Sea Grant College Program, an increase of $6.0 million (8.8%) from the FY2019 enacted amount, $1.0 million (1.4%) more than the proposed amount in H.R. 3055 and $1.0 million (1.4%) less than the proposed amount in S. 2584.[105] It also provides $13.0 million for the Marine Aquaculture Research program, an increase of $1.0 million (8.3%) from the FY2019 enacted amount and the proposed amount in H.R. 3055, and the same amount ($13.0 million) proposed in S. 2584.[106]

---

[98] Email correspondence with the NOAA Budget Office, April 8, 2019.

[99] Email correspondence with the NOAA Budget Office, January 23, 2020.

[100] Email correspondence with the NOAA Budget Office, January 23, 2020.

[101] NOAA, *Budget Estimates Fiscal Year 2020*, 2019.

[102] H.Rept. 116-9, p. 616, NOAA, *Budget Estimates Fiscal Year 2020*, 2019, and *Explanatory Statement Regarding* H.R. 1158.

[103] *Explanatory Statement Regarding* H.R. 1158, H.Rept. 116-101, pp. 29-30, and S.Rept. 116-127, pp. 46-47.

[104] NOAA, *Budget Estimates Fiscal Year 2020*, 2019.

[105] H.Rept. 116-9, p. 616, *Explanatory Statement Regarding* H.R. 1158, H.Rept. 116-101, p. 30, and S.Rept. 116-127, p. 47.

[106] H.Rept. 116-9, p. 616 and H.Rept. 116-101, pp. 30-31.

Table 15. National Oceanic and Atmospheric Administration R&D

(budget authority, in millions of dollars)

	FY2019 Enacted	FY2020 Request	FY2020 House	FY2020 Senate	FY2020 Enacted
National Ocean Service (NOS)	103.2	54.1	112.1	110.1	105.4
National Marine Fisheries Service (NMFS)	60.1	55.4	65.7	69.7	68.8
National Weather Service (NWS)	26.1	18.3	26.1	26.1	19.5
National Environmental Satellite, Data, and Information Service (NESDIS)	31.0	27.8	28.5	28.4	28.4
Office of Marine and Aviation Operations (OMAO)[a]	161.2	160.3	174.9	172.8	175.2
Office of Oceanic and Atmospheric Research (OAR)	531.4	335.1	607.2	534.0	552.6
Mission Support	25.0	0	0	0	22.0
Total R&D	**938.0**	**651.1**	**1,014.4**	**941.1**	**972.0**
NOAA, Total R&D and Non-R&D	5,424.7	4,466.5	5,489.0	5,337.3	5,352.2

Sources: Email correspondence with the NOAA Budget Office, April 8, 2019, August 5, 2019, August 8, 2019, and January 23, 2020; H.Rept. 116-9; NOAA, *Budget Estimates Fiscal Year 2020*, 2019, at https://www.corporateservices.noaa.gov/nbo/fy20_bluebook/NOAA-FY20-Congressional-Justification.pdf; H.Rept. 116-101; S.Rept. 116-127; and "Explanatory Statement Submitted by Mrs. Lowey, Chairwoman of the House Committee on Appropriations Regarding H.R. 1158, Consolidated Appropriations Act, 2020," *Congressional Record*, vol. 165, no. 204, part II (December 17, 2019).

Notes: Congress and NOAA use several budgetary terms, such as direct obligations, budget authority, and appropriations. The totals listed here are the amounts recommended by each chamber, as noted in the reports accompanying each appropriations bill (H.Rept. 116-101, S.Rept. 116-127; and Explanatory Statement Submitted by Mrs. Lowey, Chairwoman of the House Committee on Appropriations Regarding H.R. 1158, Consolidated Appropriations Act, 2020," *Congressional Record*, vol. 165, no. 204, part II (December 17, 2019)). For more information, see CRS In Focus IF11185, National Oceanic and Atmospheric Administration (NOAA): FY2020 Budget Request and Appropriations, by Eva Lipiec. Totals may differ from the sum of the components due to rounding.

a.   All Office of Marine Aviation Operations funding is for equipment related to R&D.

Department of the Interior[107]

The Department of the Interior (DOI) was created to conserve and manage the nation's natural resources and cultural heritage, to provide scientific and other information about those resources, and to uphold "the nation's trust responsibilities or special commitments to American Indians, Alaska Natives, and affiliated island communities to help them prosper." DOI has a wide range of responsibilities including, among other things, mapping, geological, hydrological, and biological science; migratory bird, wildlife, and endangered species conservation; surface-mined lands protection and restoration; and historic preservation.[108]

Because final FY2019 funding was not available at the time the FY2020 budget was prepared, requested R&D funding is compared to the FY2018 actual funding.

The Administration requested $12.6 billion in net discretionary funding for DOI in FY2020.[109] Of that amount, $757 million was requested for R&D funding, $148 million (16.3%) below the FY2018 actual level of $905 million.[110] Of the President's FY2020 DOI R&D funding request, 8.9% was for basic research, 73.3% was for applied research, and 17.8% was for development. The U.S. Geological Survey (USGS) is the only DOI component that conducts basic research.[111]

Funding for DOI R&D is generally included in appropriations line items that also include non-R&D activities. How much of the funding provided in appropriations legislation is allocated to R&D specifically is unclear unless funding is provided at the precise level of the request. In general, R&D funding levels are known only after DOI components allocate their appropriations to specific activities and report those figures.

As passed by the House on June 25, 2019, the Commerce, Justice, Science, Agriculture, Rural Development, Food and Drug Administration, Interior, Environment, Military Construction, Veterans Affairs, Transportation, and Housing and Urban Development Appropriations Act, 2020 (H.R. 3055) would have provided a total of $13.8 billion in discretionary funding for DOI, $833 million above the 2019 enacted level and $2.4 billion above the request.[112] As passed by the Senate on October 31, 2019, H.R. 3055 would also have provided a total of $13.8 billion in discretionary funding for DOI. As signed by the President on December 20, 2020, the Further Consolidated Appropriations Act, 2020 (P.L. 116-94) provided $13.9 billion for DOI, $2.1 billion more than the request, and $847 million more than the FY2019 enacted amount.[113] These amounts include both R&D and non-R&D funding.

---

[107] This section was written by Laurie Harris, Analyst in Science and Technology Policy, CRS Resources, Science, and Industry Division.

[108] Department of the Interior, *Strategic Plan for Fiscal Years 2018-2022* and *Strategic Plan for Fiscal Years 2014-2018*, available at https://www.doi.gov/performance/strategic-planning.

[109] Department of the Interior, *Fiscal Year 2020: The Interior Budget in Brief*, March 2019, p. DH-6.

[110] Email correspondence between the DOI and CRS, April 11, 2019.

[111] Ibid.

[112] House Committee on Appropriations, "H.R. 3055 Division-by-Division Summary," at https://appropriations.house.gov/sites/democrats.appropriations.house.gov/files/HR3055%20Summary_0.pdf.

[113] Explanatory Statement, Consolidated Appropriations Act, 2020, Division D (Department of the Interior, Environment, and Related Agencies Appropriations Act, 2020), *Congressional Record*, vol. 165, no. 204—Book III (December 17, 2019), p. H11333.

U.S. Geological Survey

The USGS accounts for approximately two-thirds of all DOI R&D funding. A single appropriations account, Surveys, Investigations, and Research (SIR), provides all USGS funding. USGS R&D is conducted under seven SIR activity/program areas: Ecosystems; Land Resources; Energy, Minerals, and Environmental Health; Natural Hazards; Water Resources; Core Science Systems; and Science Support.

The President's total FY2020 budget request for USGS was $984 million. Of this amount, $481 million would have been for R&D, a decrease of $119 million (19.8%) from the FY2018 enacted level of $600 million.[114]

As passed by the House, H.R. 3055 would have provided $1.236 billion for USGS, $252 million (26%) more than the FY2020 requested amount and $75.8 million (7%) more than the FY2019 enacted amount. As passed by the Senate, H.R. 3055 would have provided $1.210 billion for USGS, $226 million (23%) more than the FY2020 requested amount and $49.8 million (4%) more than the FY2019 enacted amount. P.L. 116-94 provides $1.271 billion for USGS, $288 million (29.2%) more than the requested amount, and $110 million (9.5%) more than the FY2019 enacted amount. These amounts include both R&D and non-R&D funding.

Other DOI Components

The President's FY2020 request also included R&D funding for the following DOI components:[115]

- Bureau of Reclamation (BOR): $84.0 million in applied research and development funding for FY2020, down $26.4 million (23.9%) from FY2018.

- Bureau of Ocean Energy Management (BOEM): $100.4 million in applied research and development funding for FY2020, up $22.1 million (28.2%) from FY2018—the only component that would receive an increase in R&D funding.

- Fish and Wildlife Service (FWS): $15.5 million in applied research for FY2020, down $17.2 million (52.5%) from FY2018.

- National Park Service (NPS): $25.9 million in applied research and development for FY2020, down $1.1 million (4.2%) from FY2018.

- Bureau of Safety and Environmental Enforcement (BSEE): $24.5 million in applied research for FY2020, down $2.2 million (8.2%) from FY2018.

- Bureau of Land Management (BLM): $19.0 million in applied research and development for FY2020, down $1.9 million (9.0%) from FY2018.

- Bureau of Indian Affairs (BIA): $5.0 million in applied research for FY2020, equal to the actual amount from FY2018.

- Wildland Fire Management (WFM): No funding requested for R&D for FY2020, down $3.0 million (100.0%) from FY2018.[116]

- Office of Surface Mining Reclamation and Enforcement (OSMRE): $1.5 million in applied research for FY2020, up $970,000 (190%) from FY2018.

---

[114] Ibid.

[115] Ibid.

[116] The FY2020 budget request for the Wildland Fire Management Program is $919.9 million (non-R&D funding).

Table 16 summarizes FY2018 actual R&D funding and the President's FY2020 R&D funding request for DOI components.

Table 16. Department of the Interior R&D

(budget authority, in millions of dollars)

	FY2018 Actual	FY2020 Request	FY2020 House	FY2020 Senate	FY2020 Enacted
U.S. Geological Survey (USGS)	600.5	481.4	n/s	n/s	n/s
Bureau of Reclamation (BOR)	110.5	84.0	n/s	n/s	n/s
Bureau of Ocean Energy Management (BOEM)	78.3	100.4	n/s	n/s	n/s
Fish and Wildlife Service (FWS)	32.7	15.5	n/s	n/s	n/s
National Park Service (NPS)	27.0	25.9	n/s	n/s	n/s
Bureau of Safety and Environmental Enforcement (BSEE)	26.7	24.5	n/s	n/s	n/s
Bureau of Land Management (BLM)	20.9	19.0	n/s	n/s	n/s
Bureau of Indian Affairs (BIA)	5.0	5.0	n/s	n/s	n/s
Wildland Fire Management (WFM)	3.0	0.0	n/s	n/s	n/s
Office of Surface Mining Reclamation and Enforcement (OSMRE)	0.5	1.5	n/s	n/s	n/s
Department of the Interior, R&D Total	**$905.0**	**$757.2**	**n/s**	**n/s**	**n/s**

Source: Email correspondence between the DOI and CRS, April 11, 2019.

Notes: Totals may differ from the sum of the components due to rounding. n/s = not specified.

Department of Veterans Affairs[117]

The Department of Veterans Affairs (VA) operates and maintains a national health care delivery system to provide eligible veterans with medical care, benefits, and social support. As part of the agency's mission, it seeks to advance medical R&D in areas most relevant to the diseases and conditions that affect the health care needs of veterans.

The President is proposing $1.4 billion for VA R&D in FY2020, an increase of $12 million (1%) from FY2019. (See **Table 17**.) VA R&D is funded through two accounts—the Medical and Prosthetic Research account and the Medical Care Support account. The Medical Care Support account also includes non-R&D funding, and the amount of funding that will be allocated to support R&D through appropriations legislation is unclear unless funding is provided at the precise level of the request. In general, R&D funding levels from the Medical Care Support account are only known after the VA allocates its appropriations to specific activities and reports those figures. The Medical Care Support account provides administrative and other support for

---

[117] This section was written by Marcy E. Gallo, Analyst in Science and Technology Policy, CRS Resources, Science, and Industry Division.

VA researchers and R&D projects, including infrastructure maintenance. The FY2020 request includes $762 million for VA's Medical and Prosthetic Research account, a decrease of $17 million (2%), and $648 million in funding for research supported by the agency's Medical Care Support account, an increase of $29 million (5%).

According to the President's request, FY2020 strategic priorities for VA R&D include increasing the access of veterans to clinical trials; increasing the transfer and translation of VA R&D; and "transforming VA data into a national resource" by reducing the time and effort needed to appropriately access, properly understand, and effectively use VA data for research. Clinical priorities for VA R&D in FY2020 include efforts to treat veterans at risk of suicide and research to address chronic pain and opioid addiction, posttraumatic stress disorder, traumatic brain injury, and Gulf War illness.

The Medical and Prosthetics R&D program is an intramural program managed by the Veteran Health Administration's Office of Research and Development (ORD) and conducted at VA Medical Centers and VA-approved sites nationwide. According to ORD, the mission of VA R&D is "to improve Veterans' health and well-being via basic, translational, clinical, health services, and rehabilitative research and to apply scientific knowledge to develop effective individualized care solutions for Veterans."[118] ORD consists of four main research services each headed by a director:

- Biomedical Laboratory R&D conducts preclinical research to understand life processes at the molecular, genomic, and physiological levels.

- Clinical Science R&D supports clinical trials and other human subjects research to determine the feasibility and effectiveness of new treatments such as drugs, therapies, or devices, compare existing therapies, and improve clinical care and practice.

- Health Services R&D conducts studies to identify and promote effective and efficient strategies to improve the quality and accessibility of the VA health system and patient outcomes, and to minimize health care costs.

- Rehabilitation R&D conducts research and develops novel approaches to improving the quality of life of impaired and disabled veterans.

In addition to intramural support, VA researchers are eligible to obtain funding for their research from extramural sources, including other federal agencies, private foundations and health organizations, and commercial entities. According to the President's FY2020 budget request, these additional R&D resources are estimated at $570 million in FY2020. However, unlike other federal agencies, such as the National Institutes of Health and the Department of Defense, VA does not have the authority to support extramural R&D by providing research grants to colleges, universities, or other non-VA entities.

On December 20, 2019, H.R. 1865, the Further Appropriations Act, 2020 (P.L. 116-94) was enacted. P.L. 116-94 provided $800 million for the Medical and Prosthetic Research account, an increase of $38 million (5%) above the request and $21 million (2.7%) above FY2019.

Table 17 summarizes R&D program funding for VA in the Medical and Prosthetic Research and the Medical Care Support accounts. **Table 18** details amounts to be spent in Designated Research Areas (DRAs), which VA describes as "areas of importance to our veteran patient population."

---

[118] Department of Veterans Affairs, website, "Office of Research & Development," https://www.research.va.gov/about/default.cfm.

Funding for research projects that span multiple areas may be included in several DRAs; thus, the amounts in **Table 18** total to more than the appropriation or request for VA R&D.

Table 17. Department of Veterans Affairs R&D

(budget authority, in millions of dollars)

Account	FY2019 Enacted	FY2020 Request	FY2020 House	FY2020 Senate	FY2020 Enacted
Medical and Prosthetic Research	$779.0	$762.0	$840.0	n/a	$800.0
Medical Care Support	618.3	647.7	a	n/a	a
Veterans Affairs, Total R&D	**$1,397.3**	**$1,409.7**	a	n/a	a

Source: Department of Veterans Affairs, *Volume II: Medical Programs and Information Technology Programs, Congressional Submission, FY2020 Funding and FY2021 Advance Appropriations*, p. VHA-357, https://www.va.gov/budget/docs/summary/fy2020VAbudgetVolumeIImedicalProgramsAndInformationTechnology.pdf.

Notes: Totals may differ from the sum of the components due to rounding. Figures for the column headed "FY2020 Senate" is not available (n/a); the Senate did not take action on a separate measure related to funding for the VA. VA researchers also receive grants from other federal and nonfederal resources, including the National Institutes of Health, the Department of Defense, and the Centers for Disease Control and Prevention; these resources are estimated at $570 million in FY2019 and $570 million in FY2020. Additionally, the VA estimates reimbursements associated with agency R&D at $56 million in FY2019 and $55 million in FY2020, increasing the total amount of R&D performed at VA to $2.02 billion in FY2019 and $2.03 billion in the FY2020 request.

a. Cannot be determined as R&D is included in accounts with non-R&D funding.

Table 18. Department of Veterans Affairs R&D by Designated Research Area

(in millions of dollars)

Designated Research Area	FY2019	FY2020 Request
Acute and Traumatic Injury	$25.2	$25.5
Aging	140.0	141.5
Autoimmune, Allergic, and Hematopoietic Disorders	28.8	29.1
Cancer	57.3	57.9
Central Nervous System Injury and Associated Disorders	106.2	107.3
Degenerative Diseases of Bones and Joints	37.8	38.2
Dementia and Neuronal Degeneration	33.6	34.0
Diabetes and Major Complications	40.9	41.3
Digestive Diseases	17.6	17.8
Emerging Pathogens/Bio-Terrorism	1.6	1.6
Gulf War Veterans Illness	15.0	15.0
Health Systems	75.1	75.8
Heart Disease/Cardiovascular Health	71.5	72.2
Infectious Disease	31.3	31.6
Kidney Disorders	15.9	16.1
Lung Disorders	26.0	26.3

Designated Research Area	FY2019	FY2020 Request
Mental Illness	119.1	120.4
Military Occupations and Environmental Exposures	22.9	23.1
Other Chronic Diseases	2.9	2.9
Prosthetics	19.1	19.3
Sensory Loss	15.1	15.3
Special Populations	26.8	27.1
Substance Abuse	33.0	33.3

Source: Department of Veterans Affairs, *Volume II: Medical Programs and Information Technology Programs, Congressional Submission, FY2020 Funding and FY2021 Advance Appropriations*, p. VHA-380, https://www.va.gov/budget/docs/summary/fy2020VAbudgetVolumeIImedicalProgramsAndInformationTechnology.pdf.

Notes: Projects that span multiple areas may be included in several Designated Research Areas (DRAs); therefore, the amounts depicted in this table total to more than the FY2019 amount and the FY2020 request for Medical and Prosthetic Research. Columns for "FY2020 House, "FY2020 Senate," and "FY2020 Enacted" are not included in this table as these figures will only be available after Congress completes the appropriations process and VA determines how much of the appropriated funds will be allocated to each DRA.

Department of Transportation[119]

The Department of Transportation (DOT) was established by the Department of Transportation Act (P.L. 89-670) on October 15, 1966. The primary purposes of DOT research and development activities as defined by Section 6019 of the Fixing America's Surface Transportation Act (P.L. 114-94) are improving mobility of people and goods; reducing congestion; promoting safety; improving the durability and extending the life of transportation infrastructure; preserving the environment; and preserving the existing transportation system.

Funding for DOT R&D is generally included in appropriations line items that also include non-R&D activities. The amount of the funding provided by appropriations legislation that is allocated to R&D is unclear unless funding is provided at the precise level of the request. In general, R&D funding levels are known only after DOT agencies allocate their final appropriations to specific activities and report those figures.

The Administration is requesting $1.089 billion for DOT R&D activities and facilities in FY2020, a decrease of $5.8 million (0.5%) from FY2019. (See **Table 19**.) Three DOT agencies—the Federal Aviation Administration (FAA), the Federal Highway Administration (FHWA), and the National Highway Traffic Safety Administration (NHTSA)—would account for over 90% of DOT R&D under the FY2020 request.

Federal Aviation Administration

The President's FY2020 request of $512.3 million for R&D activities and facilities at FAA would be an increase of $10.4 million (2.1%) from FY2019. The request includes $120 million for the agency's Research, Engineering, and Development (RE&D) account, a reduction of $71.1 million (37.2%) from FY2019. Funding within the RE&D account seeks to improve aircraft safety through research in fields such as fire safety, advanced materials, propulsion systems, aircraft

---

[119] This section was written by Marcy E. Gallo, Analyst in Science and Technology Policy, CRS Resources, Science, and Industry Division.

icing, and continued airworthiness, in addition to safety research related to unmanned aircraft systems and the integration of commercial space operations into the national airspace.

On December 20, 2019, H.R. 1865, the Further Appropriations Act, 2020 (P.L. 116-94) was enacted. P.L. 116-94 provide $192.7 million for the RE&D account, $1.6 million (0.8%) above FY2019 and $72.7 million (60.6%) above the request.

Federal Highway Administration

According to the President's budget request

> FHWA's contributions to researching and implementing transformative innovations and technologies are changing the way roads, bridges, and other facilities are planned, designed, built, managed, and maintained across the country to be more responsive to current and future needs.[120]

The President's request of $420 million for R&D activities and facilities at FHWA would be an increase of $39 million (10.2%) from FY2019. The request includes $125 million for FHWA's Highway Research and Development program, which seeks to improve safety, enhance the design and construction of transportation infrastructure, provide data and analysis for decisionmaking, and reduce congestion. The program supports highway research in such areas as the impact of automated driving systems, infrastructure durability, resilience, and environmental sustainability, and the factors that contribute to death and injury related to roadway design, construction, and maintenance. The request also includes $100 million for research to facilitate the development of a connected, integrated, and automated transportation system under the agency's Intelligent Transportation Systems program.

National Highway Traffic Safety Administration

The President is requesting $62.1 million in R&D and R&D facilities funding in FY2020 for NHTSA, $13.8 million (18.2%) below FY2019. NHTSA R&D focuses on automation and the study of human machine interfaces, advanced vehicle safety technology, ways of improving vehicle crashworthiness and crash avoidance, reducing unsafe driving behaviors, and alternative fuels vehicle safety.

Other DOT Components

R&D activities are also supported by several other DOT components or agencies (see **Table 19**). The President's FY2020 request includes DOT R&D and R&D facilities funding for

- the Federal Railroad Administration (FRA), totaling $23.1 million, $21.6 million (48.3%) below the FY2019 level of $44.6 million;

- the Federal Transit Administration (FTA), totaling $28 million, $2 million (6.7%) below the FY2019 level of $30 million;

- the Pipeline and Hazardous Materials Safety Administration (PHMSA), totaling $21.5 million, $3 million (12.1%) below the FY2019 level of $24.5 million;

- the Office of the Secretary (OST), totaling $13.1 million, $14.8 million (53.2%) below the FY2019 level of $27.9 million; and

---

[120] Department of Transportation, *U.S. Department of Transportation: Budget Highlights 2020*, p. 36, https://www.transportation.gov/sites/dot.gov/files/docs/mission/budget/333126/budgethighlightsfinal040519.pdf.

- the Federal Motor Carrier Safety Administration (FMCSA), totaling $9.1 million, the same amount as FY2019.

Table 19. Department of Transportation R&D Activities and Facilities

(budget authority, in millions of dollars)

	FY2019 Enacted	FY2020 Request	FY2020 House	FY2020 Senate	FY2020 Enacted
Federal Aviation Administration	$501.9	$512.3	a	a	a
Research, Engineering, and Development	*191.1*	*120.0*	*191.1*	*194.2*	*192.7*
Federal Highway Administration	381.0	420.0	a	a	a
Highway Research and Development	*112.6*	*125.0*	a	a	a
Intelligent Transportation Systems	*90.1*	*100.0*	a	a	a
National Highway Traffic Safety Administration	75.9	62.1	a	a	a
Federal Railroad Administration	44.6	23.1	a	a	a
Railroad Research and Development	*40.6*	*19.0*	*41.6*	*40.6*	*40.6*
Federal Transit Administration	30.0	28.0	a	a	a
Pipeline and Hazardous Materials Safety Administration	24.5	21.5	a	a	a
Office of the Secretary	27.9	13.1	a	a	a
Federal Motor Carrier Safety Administration	9.1	9.1	a	a	a
DOT, R&D Total	**$1,094.9**	**$1,089.1**	a	a	a

Sources: U.S. Department of Transportation, *Fiscal Year 2020 Budget Estimates*, https://www.transportation.gov/mission/budget/fiscal-year-2020-budget-estimates.

Notes: Amounts include R&D and R&D facilities. Components may not add to total due to rounding. Lines in italics are components of the agency lines above them and are not counted separately in the total. Figures for the columns headed "FY2020 House," "FY2020 Senate," and "FY2020 Enacted" will be added, if available, as each action is completed.

a. Cannot be determined, as R&D is included in accounts with non-R&D funding.

Department of Homeland Security[121]

The Department of Homeland Security (DHS) has identified five core missions: to prevent terrorism and enhance security, to secure and manage the borders, to enforce and administer immigration laws, to safeguard and secure cyberspace, and to ensure resilience to disasters. New technology resulting from research and development can contribute to achieving all these goals. The Directorate of Science and Technology (S&T) has primary responsibility for establishing, administering, and coordinating DHS R&D activities. Other components, such as the Countering Weapons of Mass Destruction Office, the U.S. Coast Guard, and the Transportation Security Administration, conduct R&D relating to their specific missions.

The President's FY2020 budget request for DHS included $438 million for activities identified as R&D. This would have been a reduction of 31.6% from $640 million in FY2019. The total included $303 million for the R&D account in the S&T Directorate and smaller amounts for five other DHS components. The House bill (H.R. 3931 as reported) would have provided $467 million, including $351 million for R&D in the S&T Directorate. The Senate bill (S. 2582 as reported) would have provided $538 million, including $416 million for R&D in the S&T Directorate. The enacted total was $546 million, including $422 million for R&D in the S&T Directorate. See **Table 20**.

The S&T Directorate performs R&D in several laboratories of its own and funds R&D performed by the DOE national laboratories, industry, universities, and others. It also conducts testing and other technology-related activities in support of acquisitions by other DHS components. The Administration's FY2020 request of $303 million for the S&T Directorate R&D account was a decrease of 40.7% from $511 million in FY2019. The request included no funding for cybersecurity R&D ($89.1 million in FY2019), which was instead to be conducted in the Cybersecurity Infrastructure Security Agency (CISA; $31 million for R&D in the FY2020 request, up from $13 million in FY2019). The remaining thrust areas in the S&T Directorate's Research, Development, and Innovation budget line were all to decrease, by amounts ranging from 12.1% (Counter Terrorist) to 40.4% (Border Security). Funding for university centers of excellence were to decrease from $37 million in FY2019 to $18 million in FY2020.

The House bill would have provided $351 million for the S&T Directorate R&D account. The House committee report recommended $24 million more than the request for cybersecurity R&D, rejecting the proposed shift of that funding from S&T to CISA. It recommended $19 million more than the request (i.e., $37 million) to continue support for 10 university centers of excellence.

The Senate bill would have provided $416 million for the S&T Directorate R&D account. The Senate committee report recommended $37 million for university centers of excellence and rejected the proposed shift of cybersecurity R&D funding from S&T to CISA, stating:

> While the Committee strongly believes that S&T should refocus its cybersecurity research to align much more closely with CISA requirements, the Committee does not believe that the Department should limit its cybersecurity research to CISA requirements alone, nor does the Committee believe that de facto transfers of research and development resources from S&T to operational components contribute to an efficient or unified Department.

The enacted appropriation for the S&T Directorate R&D account was $422 million. The final explanatory statement, like the House and Senate committee reports, rejected the shift of cybersecurity R&D funding out of the S&T Directorate to CISA. It did not specify funding for

---

[121] This section was written by Daniel Morgan, Specialist in Science and Technology Policy, CRS Resources, Science, and Industry Division.

university centers of excellence, which therefore received the $37 million recommended in the House and Senate committee reports.

In addition to its R&D account, the S&T Directorate receives funding for laboratory facilities and other R&D-related expenses through its Operations and Support account (not shown in the table). In this account, the FY2020 request for Laboratory Facilities was $116 million, down 4.9% from $122 million in FY2019. The Laboratory Facilities request included no funding for the National Urban Security Technology Laboratory, which the Administration proposed to close, or for the National Bio and Agro-Defense Facility (NBAF), which the S&T Directorate is building using previously appropriated funds but will transfer to the USDA once it becomes operational. Requested funding in Laboratory Facilities for the National Biodefense Analysis and Countermeasures Center (NBACC) was $29 million, the same as in FY2019.

The House committee report recommended $123 million for Laboratory Facilities in the S&T Operations and Support account. It stated in its discussion of the S&T Research and Development account that "funding is provided above the requested level to restore support for the National Urban Security Technology Laboratory."

The Senate committee report also recommended $123 million for Laboratory Facilities. It recommended $3.4 million—which it described as full funding—for operation of the National Urban Security Technology Laboratory.

The final explanatory statement did not specify an amount for Laboratory Facilities, which therefore received the $123 million recommended in the House and Senate committee reports. It was similarly silent regarding the National Urban Security Technology Laboratory.

The request for R&D in the Countering Weapons of Mass Destruction Office was $68 million, down from $83 million in FY2019. The House bill would have provided the requested amount. The Senate bill would have provided an additional $1.5 million in Detection Capability Development for R&D on an active neutron interrogation system. The enacted appropriation provided the $1.5 million increase described in the Senate report.

Table 20. Department of Homeland Security R&D Accounts

(budget authority, in millions of dollars)

	FY2019 Enacted	FY2020 Request	FY2020 H. Cte.	FY2020 S. Cte.	FY2020 Enacted
Science and Technology Directorate	$511	$303	$351	$416	$422
Countering Weapons of Mass Destruction Office	83	68	68	69	69
Transportation Security Administration	21	21	21	23	23
U.S. Coast Guard	20	5	5	5	5
Cybersecurity and Infrastructure Security Agency	13	31	11	9	14
Office of the Under Secretary for Management	3	—	—	—	—
U.S. Secret Service	3	11	11	16	12
Total, DHS R&D	**653**	**438**	**467**	**538**	**546**

Source: FY2020 DHS congressional budget justification, https://www.dhs.gov/publication/congressional-budget-justification-fy-2020; H.R. 3931 as reported and H.Rept. 116-180; S. 2582 as reported and S.Rept. 116-125; P.L. 116-93 and explanatory statement, *Congressional Record*, December 17, 2019, Book II.

Notes: Table includes accounts titled "Research and Development" in each DHS component. Some other accounts may also fund R&D-related activities. Some amounts may not add to totals due to rounding.

Environmental Protection Agency[122]

The U.S. Environmental Protection Agency (EPA), the federal regulatory agency responsible for administering a number of environmental pollution control laws, funds a broad range of R&D activities to provide scientific tools and knowledge that support decisions relating to preventing, regulating, and abating environmental pollution. Since FY2006, Congress has funded EPA through the Interior, Environment, and Related Agencies appropriations acts.

Appropriations for EPA R&D are generally included in line-items that also include non-R&D activities. Annual appropriations bills and the accompanying committee reports do not identify precisely how much funding provided in appropriations bills is allocated to EPA R&D alone. EPA determines its R&D funding levels in operation through allocating its appropriations to specific activities and reporting those amounts.

The agency's Science and Technology (S&T) appropriations account[123] funds much of EPA's scientific research activities, which include R&D conducted by the agency at its own laboratories and facilities, and R&D and related scientific research conducted by universities, foundations, and other nonfederal entities that receive EPA grants. The S&T account receives a base appropriation and a transfer from the Hazardous Substance Superfund (Superfund) account for research on more effective methods for remediating contaminated sites.

EPA's Office of Research and Development (ORD) is the primary manager of R&D at EPA headquarters and laboratories around the country, as well as external R&D. A large portion of the S&T account funds EPA R&D activities managed by ORD, including research grants. Programs implemented by other offices within EPA also may have a research component, but the research component is not necessarily the primary focus of the program.

Title II of Division D in the Further Consolidated Appropriations Act, 2020 (P.L. 116-94; H.R. 1865) provides $747.2 million for the EPA S&T account for FY2020 including transfers ($30.7 million) from the EPA Superfund account. The FY2020 total for the S&T account represents 8.2% of the $9.06 billion FY2020 appropriations for the agency overall.

P.L. 116-94 does not include specific rescissions of unobligated balances for EPA as in FY2019 and prior recent fiscal years' enacted appropriations.[124] The FY2019 enacted appropriations

---

[122] This section was written by Robert Esworthy, Specialist in Environmental Policy, CRS Resources, Science, and Industry Division. For an overview of EPA FY2019 and FY2020 appropriations see CRS In Focus IF11276, *U.S. EPA FY2020 Appropriations*, by Robert Esworthy, CRS In Focus IF11153, *U.S. Environmental Protection Agency (EPA) Appropriations: FY2020 President's Budget Request*, by Robert Esworthy and David M. Bearden, and CRS In Focus IF11067, *U.S. Environmental Protection Agency (EPA) FY2019 Appropriations*, by Robert Esworthy and David M. Bearden.

[123] In 1995, Congress established eight statutory accounts for EPA, including the S&T account. The S&T account incorporates elements of the former EPA Research and Development account, as well as portions of the former Salaries and Expenses and Program Operations accounts, which were in place until FY1996. Currently, including the S&T account, discretionary funding is annually appropriated to EPA among 10 statutory accounts established by Congress over time in annual appropriations acts. Because of the differences in the scope of the activities included in these accounts, comparisons before and after FY1996 are not readily available.

[124] In the Explanatory Statement accompanying P.L. 116-94, the Appropriations Committees provide a discussion of this change in Division D Title II under the heading *"Budget Rebaselining,"* Explanatory Statement, Consolidated Appropriations Act, 2019, Division D (Department of the Interior, Environment and Related Agencies Appropriations Act, 2020), *Congressional Record*, vol. 165, no. 204—Book III (December 17, 2019), p. H11291.

included account-specific rescissions for S&T and other accounts; the President's FY2020 request proposed a rescission for EPA across the board but did not specify a rescission within the S&T or other appropriations accounts. This accounting difference does not allow for direct comparisons of funding within EPA's S&T account including specific rescissions.

The FY2020 enacted appropriations for EPA's S&T account including transfers is a $266.4 million (55.4%) increase above the President's FY2020 request of $480.8 million for the account and $24.6 million (3.4%) more than the $722.6 million enacted for FY2019 (includes a $11.3 million account specific rescission and $600,000 supplemental appropriations included in P.L. 116-20 for disaster relief).

As noted earlier in this report, the House and Senate each passed versions of H.R. 3055.[125] Division C in the five-bill omnibus H.R. 3055 as passed by the House on June 25, 2019, and in the Senate 4-bill amendment to H.R. 3055 as passed by the Senate on November 4, 2019, included the Department of the Interior, Environment, and Related Agencies Appropriations Act, 2020.[126] For FY2020 Title II of Division C in House-passed H.R. 3055 would have provided $9.53 billion for EPA, including $727.6 million for the EPA S&T account. Title II of Division C in Senate-passed H.R. 3055 would have provided $9.01 billion for EPA for FY2020, including $731.0 million for the EPA S&T account for FY2020.

As with the President's FY2019 budget request, the FY2020 request proposed reductions and eliminations of funding for FY2020 across a number of EPA programs and activities, including within the S&T account.[127] The reductions proposed in the FY2020 request were distributed across EPA operational functions and activities as well as grants for states, tribes, and local governments. With the exception of the Building and Facilities account, the President's FY2020 request proposed funding reductions below FY2019 enacted levels for the nine other EPA appropriations accounts, although funding for some program areas within the accounts would remain constant or increase.

Some Members of Congress expressed concerns regarding proposed reductions of funding for EPA scientific research programs during hearings on the President's FY2020 budget request,[128] and about EPA proposals regarding the use of scientific research in agency regulatory and policy decisions.[129] Also of interest to some Members of Congress were EPA's proposed reorganizing

---

[125] The four-bill H.R. 3055 would become a the legislative vehicle for the Further Continuing Appropriations Act, 2020, and Further Health Extenders Act of 2019, P.L. 116-69 enacted November 21, 2019, which generally funded federal departments and agencies at FY2019 enacted levels through December 20, 2019.

[126] Title II of the Department of the Interior, Environment, and Related Agencies Appropriations, 2020, as reported June 3, 2019, (H.R. 3052, H.Rept. 116-100), and as reported in the Senate September 26, 2019 (S. 2580, S.Rept. 116-123), provided the basis (with some differences) for House-passed H.R. 3055 and the Senate amendment respectively.

[127] U.S. EPA, *Fiscal Year 2020 Justification of Appropriations Estimates for the Committee on Appropriations*, March 2019; "Eliminated Programs," pp. 822-827, https://www.epa.gov/planandbudget/fy-2020-justification-appropriation-estimates-committee-appropriations.

[128] U.S. Congress, House Committee on Appropriations, Subcommittee on Interior, Environment, and Related Agencies, *Budget: Environmental Protection Agency*, hearing, April 2, 2019, https://appropriations.house.gov/events/hearings/budget-environmental-protection-agency; Senate Committee on Appropriations, Subcommittee on Interior, Environment, and Related Agencies, *Review of the FY2020 Budget Request for the Environmental Protection Agency*, hearing April 3, 2019, https://www.appropriations.senate.gov/hearings/review-of-the-fy2020-budget-request-for-the-environmental-protection-agency; House Committee on Energy and Commerce, Subcommittee on Environment and Climate Change, *Hearing on "The Fiscal Year 2020 EPA Budget,"* hearing, April 9, 2019, https://energycommerce.house.gov/committee-activity/hearings/hearing-on-the-fiscal-year-2020-epa-budget.

[129] U.S. Congress, House Committee on Science, Space and Technology, *Strengthening Transparency or Silencing Science? The Future of Science in EPA Rulemaking*, hearing, November 13, 2019, https://science.house.gov/hearings/

---

strategies.[130] These proposals would potentially affect certain aspects of EPA's ORD and the operations of the EPA Office of the Science Advisor (OSA), as well as current EPA laboratories including the National Exposure Research Laboratory (NERL), the National Health and Environmental Effects Research Laboratory (NHEERL), and the National Risk Management Research Laboratory (NRMRL). Similar to the FY2019 enacted appropriations, the FY2020 enacted appropriations and the House- and Senate-passed H.R. 3055 generally did not support many of the proposed reductions and eliminations of funding for EPA, including proposed reductions in funding for scientific research programs.

Table 21 at the end of this section provides a comparison of FY2020 enacted appropriations for program areas and activities within EPA's S&T account with those amounts proposed in House- and Senate-passed H.R. 3055,[131] the President's FY2020 request, and the FY2019 enacted appropriations as reported in the Conference Report (H.Rept. 116-9) accompanying the FY2019 consolidated appropriations P.L. 116-6. As indicated in the notes accompanying the table, the FY2020 enacted appropriations below the account level are as presented in the Explanatory Statement accompanying P.L. 116-94.[132]

House and Senate Appropriations Committee reports and explanatory statements accompanying recent fiscal year EPA proposed and enacted appropriations have not specified funding for all subprogram areas reported in EPA's budget justifications. S&T subprogram areas not directly reported in House and Senate Appropriations Committee reports are noted in the **Table 21** as "NR" (not reported). Additionally, the President's FY2018, FY2019, and FY2020 requests and EPA's congressional budget justifications have modified the titles for some of the program areas relative to previous Administrations' budget requests and congressional committee reports' presentations. The House and Senate Appropriations Committees have generally adopted the modified program area titles as presented in the recent budget requests.

As indicated in the table, with the exception of adjusting for "budget reshaping" (rescissions) discussed earlier,[133] the enacted FY2020 appropriations generally would be the same or an increase above the FY2019 enacted appropriations. With the exception of "Operations and Administration," the proposed amounts would be an increase compared to the FY2020 requested

---

strengthening-transparency-or-silencing-science-the-future-of-science-in-epa-rulemaking.

[130] U.S. EPA, "EPA's Office of Research and Development Reorganizes to Better Support EPA's Mission," April 8, 2019, press release, https://www.epa.gov/sciencematters/epas-office-research-and-development-reorganizes-better-support-epas-mission.

[131] U.S. Congress, House Committee on Appropriations, *Department of the Interior, Environment and Related Agencies Appropriations Bill, 2020*, report to accompany H.R. 3052 as reported, 116th Cong., 1st sess., H.Rept. 116-100 (Washington, DC: GPO, 2019), pp. 78-83; H.R. 3055 Title II, Division C includes references to H.Rept. 116-100 for specific guidance regarding the administration of certain appropriated funds. Senate Committee on Appropriations, *Department of the Interior, Environment and Related Agencies Appropriations Bill, 2020*, report to accompany S. 2580 as reported, 116th Cong., 1st sess. S.Rept. 116-123 (Washington, DC: GPO, 2019), pp. 71-98. "References to Report" in Section 3(a) of the Senate amendment to H.R. 3055, specifies that any reference to a "report accompanying this Act" in Division C refers to S.Rept. 116-123.

[132] *Congressional Record*, vol. 165, no. 204—Book III (December 17, 2019), see pp. H11281-11297; Funding Tables, pp. H11298-11360, https://www.govinfo.gov/content/pkg/CREC-2019-12-17/pdf/CREC-2019-12-17-house-bk3.pdf.

[133] The FY2020 enacted appropriations (see footnote 124), House-passed H.R. 3055 and the Senate-passed amendment did not include account-specific rescissions as in FY2019 and prior fiscal year appropriations. House and Senate Appropriations Committees noted that their consideration of the FY2020 appropriations for EPA's S&T program activities accounted for funding amounts reported in EPA's operating plan for FY2019 that reflect rescission reductions. See additional discussion in H.Rept. 116-100 accompanying H.R. 3052 as reported, and S.Rept. 116-123 accompanying S. 2580 as reported; for example, see discussion under the heading "Budget Rebaselining" beginning on p. 73 of the Senate Committee report S.Rept. 116-123.

levels. For other program areas, proposed reductions in requested funding included eliminations of certain EPA programs. For example, the proposed reduction in funding for Research: Air and Energy, Research: Safe and Sustainable Water Resources, Research: Sustainable and Healthy Communities, and Research: Chemical Safety and Sustainability program areas for FY2020[134] included the proposed elimination of funding for the Science to Achieve Results (STAR) program.[135] The FY2020 enacted appropriations, and the House- and Senate-passed H.R. 3055 rejected these proposed eliminations.

The FY2020 enacted appropriations for the S&T account includes $6.0 million for Research: National Priorities within the S&T account for FY2020,[136] an increase compared to $5.0 million included for FY2019. As in the previous Administration's fiscal year requests, the President's FY2020 budget request did not include funding for Research: National Priorities.[137]

In addition to clarifying certain FY2020 funding allocations within the EPA S&T account and consistent with the prior fiscal year appropriations the Explanatory Statement accompanying P.L. 116-94 provides additional guidance for program areas and activities within the S&T account for FY2020, including references to discussion as presented H.Rept. 116-100 accompanying H.R. 3052 as reported June 3, 2019, and S.Rept. 116-123 accompanying S. 2580 as reported September 26, 2019.[138]

Table 21. U.S. Environmental Protection Agency Science and Technology (S&T) Account

(appropriations, in millions of dollars)

S&T Program Areas/Activities	FY2019 Enacted	FY2020 Request	FY2020 House	FY2020 Senate	FY2020 Enacted
Clean Air [and Climate]ª	$116.5	$87.3	$117.2	$115.4	$116.1
Clean Air Allowance Trading Program	NR	5.7	NR	NR	NR
*Atmospheric Protection Program [GHG (greenhouse gas) Reporting Program; and Climate Protection Program]*ª	8.0	0.0	8.0	7.8	7.8
Federal Support for Air Quality Management	NR	3.8	NR	NR	NR
Federal Vehicle and Fuel Standards and Certification	NR	77.8	NR	NR	NR
Enforcement (Forensics Support)	13.7	10.9	14.7	13.0	13.6

---

[134] For a description of the activities included under this program activity within EPA's S&T account, see the agency's FY2020 Congressional budget justification, U.S. EPA, *Fiscal Year 2020 Justification of Appropriations Estimates for the Committee on Appropriation*, pp. 115-120.

[135] See discussion under the heading "FY 2020 Change from FY 2019 Annualized Continuing Resolution (Dollars in Thousands)" within this program area in U.S. EPA, *Fiscal Year 2020 Justification of Appropriations Estimates for the Committee on Appropriation*, pp. 113, 120, 126, and 132. See also, discussion under "Eliminated Programs" pp. 822-827.

[136] The grants would be independent of the Science to Achieve Results (STAR) grant program. The grants would be subject to a 25% matching funds requirement as stipulated in H.Rept. 116-100 accompanying H.R. 3052 as reported (June 3, 2019), p. 81, as referenced in H.R. 3055, Title II, Division C, and S.Rept. 116-123 accompanying S. 2580 as reported (September 26, 2019) p. 76, as referenced in Title II, Division C in the Senate amendment to H.R. 3055.

[137] Referred to as "Congressional Priorities" in U.S. EPA *Fiscal Year 2020 Justification of Appropriations Estimates for the Committee on Appropriation*. Not requesting funding for this program is consistent with the previous Administration's fiscal year budget requests.

[138] See footnote 131.

S&T Program Areas/Activities	FY2019 Enacted	FY2020 Request	FY2020 House	FY2020 Senate	FY2020 Enacted
Homeland Security	33.1	32.8	34.4	33.1	33.1
Critical Infrastructure Protection	*NR*	*7.5*	*NR*	*NR*	*NR*
Preparedness, Response, and Recovery	*NR*	*24.8*	*NR*	*NR*	*NR*
Protection of EPA Personnel and Infrastructure	*NR*	*0.5*	*NR*	*NR*	*NR*
Indoor Air and Radiation	6.0	4.8	6.0	5.1	5.1
Indoor Air: Radon Program	*NR*	*0.0*	*NR*	*NR*	*NR*
Radiation: Protection	*NR*	*1.0*	*NR*	*NR*	*NR*
Radiation: Response Preparedness	*NR*	*3.8*	*NR*	*NR*	*NR*
Reduce Risks from Indoor Air	*NR*	*0.0*	*NR*	*NR*	*NR*
Information Technology/Data Management/Security	3.1	2.7	2.7	3.1	3.1
Operations and Administration	68.3	73.3	67.3	67.5	65.4
Facilities Infrastructure and Operations	*NR*	*67.2*	*NR*	*NR*	*NR*
Workforce Reshaping[b]	*0.0*	*6.0*	*0.0*	*0.0*	*0.0*
Pesticide Licensing	6.0	5.3	5.3	5.9	5.9
Protect Human Health from Pesticide Risk	*NR*	*2.4*	*NR*	*NR*	*NR*
Protect the Environment. from Pesticide Risk	*NR*	*2.3*	*NR*	*NR*	*NR*
Realize the Value of Pesticide Availability	*NR*	*0.6*	*NR*	*NR*	*NR*
Research: Air [Climate] and Energy[a]	94.9	31.7	95.4	94.5	94.5
Research: Chemical Safety and Sustainability	126.9	86.6	126.9	126.3	126.3
Human Health Risk Assessment	*NR*	*22.7*	*NR*	*NR*	*NR*
Research: Computational Toxicology	*21.4*	*17.6*	*21.4*	*21.4*	*NR*
Research: Endocrine Disruptor	*16.3*	*10.3*	*16.3*	*16.3*	*NR*
Research: Other Activities	*NR*	*35.9*	*NR*	*NR*	*NR*
Research: Safe and Sustainable Water Resources	106.3	70.0	113.3	106.9	110.9
Research: Sustainable and Healthy Communities	134.3	53.6	134.3	132.5	132.5
Water: Human Health Protection (Drinking Water Programs)	3.5	4.1	4.1	4.1	4.1
Research: National/Congressional Priorities (Water Quality and Support Grants)[c]	5.0	0.0	6.0	6.0	6.0
Subtotal Base Appropriations	**717.7**	**463.1**	**727.6**	**713.3**	**716.4**
Transfer in from Hazardous Substance Superfund Account	**15.5**	**17.8**	**30.5**	**17.8**	**30.7**
Total Appropriations Prior to Rescissions	**733.2**	**480.8**	**758.1**	**731.0**	**747.2**
S&T Account-Specific Rescission	**(11.3)[d]**	**NR[e]**	**0[f]**	**0[f]**	**0[f]**
Supplemental Appropriations	**0.6[g]**	**N/A**	**N/A**	**N/A**	**N/A**
Total (Net Appropriations)	**722.6**	**480.8**	**758.1**	**731.0**	**747.2**

Source: Prepared by CRS using information from the *Congressional Record*; House, Senate committee reports and explanatory statements; information from the House and Senate Appropriations Committees; and EPA's *Fiscal Year 2020 Justification of Appropriations Estimates for the Committee on Appropriations*, March 2019.

Notes: Totals may differ from the sum of the components due to rounding. NR (not reported) indicates those instances where funding or rescission ("cancelled") amounts were not specified, N/A=not applicable.

a. Brackets [ ] denote title language as presented in previous Administrations' EPA budget justifications and congressional reports/explanatory statements.

b. This program activity was included in multiple EPA accounts in the FY2018, FY2019, and FY2020 budget justifications and had not been included in previous fiscal year EPA budget justifications, and not supported in House and Senate committee reports and explanatory statements accompanying appropriations.

c. Referred to as "Congressional Priorities" in the FY2020 and previous Administrations' budget justifications.

d. The Conference Report (H.Rept. 116-9) accompanying the FY2019 enacted appropriations noted that EPA's current workforce was below prior levels and therefore included separate rescissions within the S&T and the Environmental Programs and Management (EPM) accounts to "capture expected savings associated with such changes." As specified in the act, the rescission within the S&T account was not to be applied to "Research: National Priorities." House- and Senate-passed H.R. 3055, and P.L. 116-94 did not include account-specific rescissions as in previous recent fiscal year EPA appropriations.

e. The President's FY2020 request included a $227.0 million rescission of unobligated balances for EPA appropriations overall but did not specify a proportional allocation of the rescission by EPA accounts.

f. P.L. 116-94, and House and Senate-passed H.R. 3055 did not include specific rescissions of unobligated balances for EPA as in FY2019 and prior recent fiscal years' enacted appropriations. In the Explanatory Statement accompanying P.L. 116-94, the Appropriations Committees provide a discussion of this change in Division D Title II under the heading "Budget Rebaselining," Explanatory Statement, Consolidated Appropriations Act, 2019, Division D (Department of the Interior, Environment and Related Agencies Appropriations Act, 2020), *Congressional Record*, vol. 165, no. 204—Book III (December 17, 2019), p. H11291. H.R. 3055 as passed by the House on May 22, 2019, and the amendment passed by the Senate September 26, 2019 refer to this discussion as included H.Rept. 116-100 accompanying H.R. 3052 as reported June 3, 2019 and S.Rept. 116-123 accompanying S. 2580 as reported September 26, 2019.

g. P.L. 116-20, the Additional Supplemental Appropriations for Disaster Relief Act, 2019, included $600,000 for EPA's S&T account for necessary expenses related to improving preparedness of the water sector.

Appendix A. Acronyms and Abbreviations

Acronym/ Abbreviation	Organization/Term
ACF	Administration for Children and Families
AFRI	Agriculture and Food Research Initiative
AHRQ	Agency for Healthcare Research and Quality
AI	Artificial Intelligence
AIMS	Arctic Infrastructure Modernization for Science
AMP	Advanced Manufacturing Partnership – or – Accelerating Medicines Partnership
AOAM	Agency Operations and Award Management
APHIS	Animal and Plant Health Inspection Service
ARPA-E	Advanced Research Projects Agency-Energy
ARS	Agricultural Research Service
B&F	Buildings and Facilities
BA	Budget Authority
BIA	Bureau of Indian Affairs
BLM	Bureau of Land Management
BOEM	Bureau of Ocean Energy Management
BOR	Bureau of Reclamation
BRAIN	Brain Research through Advancing Innovative Neurotechnologies
BSEE	Bureau of Safety and Environmental Enforcement
CDC	Centers for Disease Control and Prevention
CLARREO	Climate Absolute Radiance and Refractivity Observatory
CMS	Centers for Medicare and Medicaid Services
CR	Continuing Resolution
CRF	Construction of Research Facilities
DHP	Defense Health Program
DHS	Department of Homeland Security
DOC	Department of Commerce
DOD	Department of Defense
DOE	Department of Energy
DOI	Department of the Interior
DOT	Department of Transportation
DRA	Designated Research Area
EHR	Education and Human Resources
EOP	Executive Office of the President
EPA	Environmental Protection Agency
EPM	Environmental Programs and Management

Acronym/ Abbreviation	Organization/Term
EPSCoR	Experimental Program to Stimulate Competitive Research –or– Established Program to Stimulate Competitive Research
ERS	Economic Research Service
FAA	Federal Aviation Administration
FDA	Food and Drug Administration
FHWA	Federal Highway Administration
FIC	Fogarty International Center
FMCSA	Federal Motor Carrier Safety Administration
FRA	Federal Railroad Administration
FTA	Federal Transit Administration
FWS	Fish and Wildlife Service
FY	Fiscal Year
GDP	Gross Domestic Product
GHG	greenhouse gas
GRF	Graduate Research Fellowship
GWOT	Global War on Terror
HBCU	Historically Black Colleges and Universities
HEAL	Helping to End Addiction Long-Term
HHS	Department of Health and Human Services
HRSA	Health Resources and Services Administration
ICs	Institutes and Centers
IDeA	Institutional Development Award
IFF	Iraqi Freedom Fund
IRIS	Integrated Risk Information System
ISS	International Space Station
ITER	International Thermonuclear Experimental Reactor
ITS	Industrial Technology Services
JWST	James Webb Space Telescope
LEO	Low Earth Orbit
LHHS	Labor, HHS, and Education appropriations act
LSST	Large Synoptic Survey Telescope
MEP	Manufacturing Extension Partnership
MGI	Materials Genome Initiative
MREFC	Major Research Equipment and Facilities Construction
NASA	National Aeronautics and Space Administration
NASS	National Agricultural Statistics Service

Acronym/ Abbreviation	Organization/Term
NBACC	National Biodefense Analysis and Countermeasures Center
NBAF	National Bio and Agro-Defense Facility
NCATS	National Center for Advancing Translational Sciences
NCCIH	National Center for Complementary and Integrative Health
NCI	National Cancer Institute
NEI	National Eye Institute
NERL	National Exposure Research Laboratory
NESDIS	National Environmental Satellite, Data, and Information Service
NHEERL	National Health and Environmental Effects Research Laboratory
NHGRI	National Human Genome Research Institute
NHLBI	National Heart, Lung, and Blood Institute
NHTSA	National Highway Traffic Safety Administration
NIA	National Institute on Aging
NIAAA	National Institute on Alcohol Abuse and Alcoholism
NIAID	National Institute of Allergy and Infectious Diseases
NIAMS	National Institute of Arthritis and Musculoskeletal and Skin Diseases
NIBIB	National Institute of Biomedical Imaging and Bioengineering
NICHD	National Institute of Child Health and Human Development
NIDA	National Institute on Drug Abuse
NIDCD	National Institute on Deafness and Other Communication Disorders
NIDCR	National Institute of Dental and Craniofacial Research
NIDDK	National Institute of Diabetes and Digestive and Kidney Diseases
NIEHS	National Institute of Environmental Health Sciences
NIFA	National Institute of Food and Agriculture
NIGMS	National Institute of General Medical Sciences
NIH	National Institutes of Health
NIIMBL	National Institute for Innovation in Manufacturing Biopharmaceuticals
NIMH	National Institute of Mental Health
NIMHD	National Institute on Minority Health and Health Disparities
NINDS	National Institute of Neurological Disorders and Stroke
NINR	National Institute of Nursing Research
NIRSQ	National Institute for Research on Safety and Quality
NIST	National Institute of Standards and Technology
NITRD	Networking and Information Technology Research and Development
NLM	National Library of Medicine
NMFS	National Marine Fisheries Service

Acronym/ Abbreviation	Organization/Term
NNI	National Nanotechnology Initiative
NNMI	National Network for Manufacturing Innovation
NOAA	National Oceanic and Atmospheric Administration
NOS	National Ocean Service
NPS	National Park Service
NRI	National Robotics Initiative
NRMRL	National Risk Management Research Laboratory
NRT	NSF Research Traineeships
NSB	National Science Board
NSET	Nanoscale Science, Engineering, and Technology (NSTC Subcommittee)
NSF	National Science Foundation
NSTC	National Science and Technology Council
NWS	National Weather Service
OAR	Oceanic and Atmospheric Research
OCO	Overseas Contingency Operations
OD	NIH Office of the Director
OIG	Office of the Inspector General
OMAO	Office of Marine and Aviation Operations
OMB	Office of Management and Budget
ORD	Office of Research and Development
OSMRE	Office of Surface Mining Reclamation and Enforcement
OST	Office of the Secretary of Transportation
OSTP	Office of Science and Technology Policy
PACE	Pre-Aerosol, Clouds, and Ocean Ecosystem
PCORTF	Patient-Centered Outcomes Research Trust Fund
PE	Program Element
PHMSA	Pipeline and Hazardous Materials Safety Administration
PHS	Public Health Service
PMI	Precision Medicine Initiative
R&D	Research and Development
RDT&E	Research, Development, Test, and Evaluation
RE&D	Research, Engineering, and Development
REE	Research, Education, and Economics
RPG	Research Project Grant
RRA	Research and Related Activities
S&T	Science and Technology

Acronym/ Abbreviation	Organization/Term
SIR	Surveys, Investigations, and Research
SLS	Space Launch System
STAG	State and Tribal Assistance Grants
STAR	Science to Achieve Results
STEM	Science, Technology, Engineering, and Mathematics
STEP	Supercritical Transformational Electric Power
STRS	Scientific and Technical Research and Services
TOA	Total Obligational Authority
USDA	Department of Agriculture
USGCRP	U.S. Global Change Research Program
USGS	U.S. Geological Survey
VA	Department of Veterans Affairs
WFIRST	Wide Field Infrared Space Telescope
WFM	Wildland Fire Management

Appendix B. CRS Contacts for Agency R&D

The following table lists the primary CRS experts on R&D funding for the agencies covered in this report.

Agency	CRS Contact
Department of Agriculture	Tadlock Cowan Specialist in Agricultural Policy
Department of Commerce	
National Institute of Standards and Technology	John F. Sargent Jr., Coordinator Specialist in Science and Technology Policy
National Oceanic and Atmospheric Administration	Eva Lipiec Analyst in Natural Resources Policy
Department of Defense	John F. Sargent Jr., Coordinator Specialist in Science and Technology Policy
Department of Energy	Daniel Morgan Specialist in Science and Technology Policy
Department of Health and Human Services National Institutes of Health	Kavya Sekar Analyst in Health Policy
Department of Homeland Security	Daniel Morgan Specialist in Science and Technology Policy
Department of the Interior	Laurie A. Harris Analyst in Science and Technology Policy
Department of Transportation	Marcy E. Gallo Analyst in Science and Technology Policy
Department of Veterans Affairs	Marcy E. Gallo Analyst in Science and Technology Policy
Environmental Protection Agency	Robert Esworthy Specialist in Environmental Policy
National Aeronautics and Space Administration	Daniel Morgan Specialist in Science and Technology Policy
National Science Foundation	Laurie A. Harris Analyst in Science and Technology Policy

Author Information

John F. Sargent Jr., Coordinator
Specialist in Science and Technology Policy

Tadlock Cowan
Analyst in Natural Resources and Rural
Development

Robert Esworthy
Specialist in Environmental Policy

Marcy E. Gallo
Analyst in Science and Technology Policy

Laurie A. Harris
Analyst in Science and Technology Policy

Eva Lipiec
Analyst in Natural Resources Policy

Daniel Morgan
Specialist in Science and Technology Policy

Kavya Sekar
Analyst in Health Policy

Disclaimer

This document was prepared by the Congressional Research Service (CRS). CRS serves as nonpartisan shared staff to congressional committees and Members of Congress. It operates solely at the behest of and under the direction of Congress. Information in a CRS Report should not be relied upon for purposes other than public understanding of information that has been provided by CRS to Members of Congress in connection with CRS's institutional role. CRS Reports, as a work of the United States Government, are not subject to copyright protection in the United States. Any CRS Report may be reproduced and distributed in its entirety without permission from CRS. However, as a CRS Report may include copyrighted images or material from a third party, you may need to obtain the permission of the copyright holder if you wish to copy or otherwise use copyrighted material.

www.ingramcontent.com/pod-product-compliance
Lightning Source LLC
Chambersburg PA
CBHW081627250726
48657CB00009B/2768